Shaping Organisational Strategies

Shaping Organisational Strategies

——— ❖ ———

Future Perspectives, Concepts and Cases

Gautam Raj Jain
Atul Tandan

Response Books
A division of Sage Publications
New Delhi ❖ Thousand Oaks ❖ London

First published in 2006 by

Response Books
A division of Sage Publications India Pvt. Ltd
B-42, Panchsheel Enclave
New Delhi 110 017

SAGE Publications Inc	**SAGE Publications Ltd**
2455 Teller Road	1 Oliver's Yard,
Thousand Oaks,	55 City Road
California 91320	London EC1Y 1SP

Published by Vivek Mehra for SAGE Publications India Pvt Ltd, typeset in 10/13 pt BruceOldStyle BT by Star Compugraphics Private Limited, Delhi and printed at Chaman Enterprises, New Delhi.

Library of Congress Cataloging-in-Publication Data

Third Printing 2012

Jain, Gautam Raj.
  Shaping organisational strategies: future perspectives, concepts and cases/ Gautam Raj Jain, Atul Tandan.
    p. cm.
  Includes bibliographical references and index.
  1. Management. I. Tandan, Atul, 1948– II. Title
  HD31 .J2453   658.4'012—dc22   2006   2006011242

ISBN: 10: 0-7619-3382-4 (HB)   10: 81-7829-651-0 (India–HB)
         13: 978-0-7619-3382-3 (HB)   13: 978-81-7829-651-7 (India–HB)
         10: 0-7619-3393-X (PB)   10: 81-7829-652-7 (India–PB)
         13: 978-0-7619-3393-9 (PB)   13: 978-81-7829-652-4 (India–PB)

Production Team: Payal Mehta, Anindita Pandey, R.A.M. Brown and Santosh Rawat

❖

To my father,
Late Shri Bipin Bihari Tandan,
For inculcating values
of study and introspection

Contents

❖

Abbreviations

———— ❖ ————

B-school	–	Business School
HBR	–	Harvard Business Review
OB	–	Organisational Behaviour
ODy	–	Organisational Dynamics
SARS	–	Severe Acute Respiratory Syndrome
UN	–	United Nations
4P	–	Popeye Pizza Parlour Private Ltd
AHT	–	Average Handling Time
ATC	_	Air Traffic Control
BMC	–	Blaze Motor Corporation
BPO	–	Business Process Outsourcing
CAT	–	Common Admissions Test
Cdr	–	Commander
CEO	–	Chief Executive Officer
CMDP	–	Corporate Management Development Programme
CRM	–	Customer Relationship Management
CT	–	Computed Tomography
DGM	–	Deputy General Manager
EMD	–	Export Marketing Division
FMCG	–	Fast Moving Consumer Goods
FRMC	–	Financial Research and Marketing Company
GI	–	Gas India
GM	–	General Manager
GMI	–	Gujarat Management Institute
HOC	–	Hindustan Oil Corporation
HR	–	Human Resources
IBD	–	International Business Development

IIT	–	Indian Institute of Technology
ISL	–	Indica Steel Limited
ISMA	–	Indian School of Management, Ahmedabad
IT	–	Information Technology
KSP	–	Kubera Steel Plant in Jharkhand
LME	–	Lifesavers Medical Equipment
LSP	–	Longewaad Steel Plant in Maharashtra
Ltd	–	Limited
MBA	–	Masters in Business Administration
MNC	–	Multi-National Company
MTI	–	Management Training Institute
NGO	–	Non-Governmental Organisation
NMO	–	National Marketing Organisation
NPA	–	Non-Performing Asset
NRI	–	Non-resident Indian
NST	–	New Solutions Technology
PCC	–	Planning and Control Department
PG	–	Post Graduate
PL	–	Project Leader
PSU	–	Public Sector Unit
Pvt.	–	Private
RSM	–	Regional Sales Manager
RSP	–	Rasagarh Steel Plant in Chhatisgarh
SDL	–	System Delivery Leader
SEWA	–	Self-Employed Women's Association
TL	–	Team Leader
TV	–	Television
UK	–	United Kingdom
USA	–	United States of America

Cases

❖

Foreword

Tens of thousands of students graduate from our management schools, most of them without any significant prior work experience. At school they learn various tools and techniques for arriving at 'optimal' decisions, modes of economic and behavioural analysis, and the basics of strategic and functional management. Thus armed, they go forth into the real world, mostly at the bottom of the managerial ladder. They quickly discover how inadequate is what they have learnt about management. More often than not, they find themselves, not as decision makers but as pawns of decision makers. The agendas of these decision-makers usually go beyond making decisions in the best interests of the organisation to personal ambitions, doing favours and extracting favours, getting even, forming or strengthening cliques or undermining cliques that oppose theirs, manipulating the power structure for personal ends, and so forth. More rarely there are contests about ideological and policy issues, values, vision, and strategy. There is a big disconnect between how managers are supposed to function and how they actually do.

The neophytes also find that the organisation is not as solid and well designed as it seems. There are frequently powerful positions not formally on the organisation chart, and high positions on the chart that are devoid of power. Then there are organisational shocks like sudden transfers, policy shifts, and strategic and structural changes that make no apparent sense. Occasionally, young managers inhale the stench of corruption or other unethical action without a clue as to how to respond. Our young friends feel helpless because the curriculum has not equipped them to deal with all these organisational dynamics.

Eventually, of course, the young manager learns the ropes, but at the cost of much disillusionment and after undergoing many traumatic experiences and blundering into blind alleys. This book seeks to sensitise students to organisational dynamics *before* they join the ranks of management. Studying it can enable them to make far better sense of ground realities, and to chart their career paths and make their organisational contributions at lesser personal cost and with greater effectiveness.

The book seeks to do much more. It explains—and illustrates with numerous indigenous cases—how organisations and their stakeholders are impacted by a rapidly liberalising and globalising business arena, and how environmental flux is challenging established notions of how organisations should be designed and how they should operate. It alerts them to the fact that 'speed, innovation, short cycle of products and services, quality, customer satisfaction, and growth of intangible assets have become a way of organisational life....', and further that 'the fast pace of change in the global market on account of information and communication technology requires organisations to constantly evolve new modes of management practices in order to remain competitive' (see Introduction). The book challenges the reader to try and make sense of complex situations, that is, mentally construct organisational models on their own as part of a 'grounded theory' enterprise. This feature of the book makes it especially suitable also to the practitioner struggling with complex, multidimensional, and confusing ground realities.

The book has many strengths. The language is lucid and relatively free of jargon. Unlike most books in the broad area of Organisational Behaviour, it incorporates rich contributions by the students themselves, in the form of cases. Both the distinguished authors bring to the table rich and varied personal experiences as practitioners *and* academics, a relatively rare combination. The cases are fascinating snapshots of organisational life, albeit somewhat restricted because they are from the Ahmedabad area. Together, they constitute quite a display of how organisations function. Each chapter indicates to the reader what is supposed to be learnt, provides a useful review of relevant concepts and models, lists some challenging learning opportunities and discusses several cases that provide enough puzzlement to invite excited analysis from multiple perspectives.

Kudos is due to the two authors for an excellent contribution to the field of organisational dynamics.

Pradip N. Khandwalla

Acknowledgements

❖

The authors would like to thank the 69 students of MICA's Post Graduate Course in Communications Management (2004–5 batch) for contributing to the basis for this book by way of developing the 33 cases. The students' edit team comprising Noopur Keswani, Anshul Sushil, Joypratip Sengupta, Gautam Jain, Gaurava Singh and Rohitash Srivastava helped in the initial preparation of the manuscript by coordinating and compiling the cases.

We also thank Jalp Lakia, designer at MICA, for the layout and design of the manuscript for internal circulation and Esha Patnaik, communications professional, for editing and assisting in revising the final draft of the manuscript.

1

❖

introduction

Expected Learning Outcomes

♦ *Identify issues associated with behaviour-oriented courses in a management school.*

♦ *Appreciate the need for educational innovations in management schools.*

♦ *Comprehend the distinction between learning plans in OB courses based on past theories and practices and ODy courses on current and future needs of organisations.*

genesis

Since the inception of management education in India, a set of courses in Organisational Behaviour (OB) has been offered as part of the traditional B school curriculum. However, increasing indifference of students towards the subject has been observed in recent times. The authors of this book were puzzled over the conflicting responses. On the one hand, students enjoyed the behavioural games and exercises that were conducted in OB sessions and on the other, they questioned, 'Does the learning have any practical application?'. They could not see the relevance of what is taught in class to the role of a manager. Contrary to this, practising managers have been continuously demanding courses or programmes that would help them deal effectively with internal dynamics. The difficulty is not one of students not being serious about the subject, but of being unable to find practical application of the learning from the sessions for improving their managerial effectiveness. As a result of this, many prospective managers may enter the corporate world without being sensitive to the dynamics of organisational functioning. They may also lack the ability to deal with their personal and interpersonal dynamics.

The students' feedback forced the authors to take a serious look at the OB course structure, its contents and pedagogy, and in the process also review available literature on management education. One study on the curriculum review of B schools revealed that some of the subjects actually developed bureaucratic behaviour among future managers rather than make them dynamic and spontaneous. Students tended to structure organisational and management practices into predetermined sets of roles and techniques (Mintzberg and Gosling, 2002; Patel and Jain, 1991).

Both students and instructors are of the view that the OB syllabus is losing relevance in the current organisational environment. The analysis of the curriculum indicated that what was being taught to management graduates were age-old theories and practices of the past, and cases and exercises developed in Western countries (Nevins and Stumpf, 1999). OB courses need to incorporate current realities of business organisations which have shifted to a new economic paradigm. Speed, innovation, short cycle of products and services, quality, customer satisfaction and growth of intangible assets have become a way of organisational life (Harvey and Buckley, 2002). Further, the fast pace of change in the global market on account of information and communication technology requires organisations to constantly evolve new models of management practices in order to remain competitive.

Given the constant shifts and changes occurring in the business environment and the need for organisations to adapt to such changes, courses in OB have to go beyond past models of organisational practices and develop an educational pedagogy that facilitates students' learning through experiencing current organisational realities. The purpose is to equip students with the capacity to foresee and conceptualise possible practices for dealing with organisational dynamics rather than just learn organisational behaviour, to keep pace with the challenges of the global market economy.

a new paradigm of learning in organisational dynamics

For the authors, OB is a subject that structures and limits the behaviour of students around certain age-old theories of behavioural sciences. As opposed to this, the main purpose of the new course on 'organisational dynamics' (ODy) is to develop a dynamic mind that enables students to discover complex but ever-changing patterns of relationship of the people with the organisational systems and its contextual environment, and respond to them creatively.

The thrust of the course was to initiate students to be self-learners and generate knowledge based on current trends and practices in dealing with organisational dynamics. As per the pedagogy of the course, students were engaged in self-exploration to find the ground realities of the organisations, dynamics at the workplace and what sustained the managers' urge to remain dynamic or organic rather than bureaucratic, mechanical or structured in dealing with business challenges. Small groups of students visited various organisations in Ahmedabad and discussed issues that organisations and managers currently faced. They discussed their experiences in the first session of the course. Their learning from the visit reinforced the importance of organisational dynamics issues and encouraged them for further enquiry.

The pedagogy of the course necessitated both the instructors and students to assume new roles. Students, as opposed to the instructors alone, were considered potential sources for generating knowledge. The instructors assumed the new role of a learner rather than just acting as the learned. In order to facilitate mutual learning, the challenge for instructors was to deal with the dynamics of students inside and outside the classroom. In addition, the instructors had to play the role of a manager to manage 60-odd students for their active participation in the creation of new knowledge and conversion of that knowledge into a case study format. Enthusiastic about providing a new and fresh insight into organisational dynamics, teams of students undertook field projects to document their experiences by writing cases in organisational dynamics. Students worked, inspired and motivated one another to prepare cases which were of publishable standards. The motivation of students was so high that some teams wanted to write more cases beyond the requirement of the course. The outcome of this unique education experience was not only the publication of this book, but also established the fact that students themselves are an effective source of knowledge generation.

OBJECTIVES AND FRAMEWORK OF THE BOOK

The book comprises cases in ODy covering a host of situations that organisations and managers experience while dealing with or responding to internal and external environmental constraints. These cases are based on real life situations involving a series of interactions and interviews with managers at different levels of the organisations. These cases provide insight into the contemporary approaches of managers and organisations with regard to changes under the new economic paradigm.

The cases have been grouped into several modules on the basis of the aspects of organisational dynamics that they cover. Accordingly, the concepts discussed in the book have emerged out of this classification. The concepts are not based on a particular theoretical framework but broadly discuss the emerging issues and thrust of the cases. Each module gives an introduction to the concept, followed by a set of cases that illustrate that concept.

The book presents the case method as an important learning pedagogy for dealing with organisational dynamics creatively. The authors consider that if the case analysis is based on a structured framework, it may limit learning as it reinforces the same set of dimensions of a theory or framework of analysis already selected. This approach may, therefore, hinder the development of a dynamic mind.

The main learning process that the book offers is based on 'learning through experiencing'. Learners have to involve themselves in developing their own perspective and deeper insights through self-reflection. The approach prompts the use of imagination in diagnosing and conceptualising the issues and drawing possible implications for various aspects of organisational functioning. The main objective of the book is, therefore, to help build a perspective about various organisational situations rather than apply a set of strategies or theoretical framework for analysing organisational dynamics.

target audience and structure

The book will be useful for prospective as well as practising managers to gain deeper insight and understanding of issues of organisational dynamics and evolve approaches to deal with them efficiently and creatively. Educational and training institutes may use these cases as part of the learning pedagogy in sessions related to organisational behaviour, and personal and interpersonal dynamics.

The book is divided into eight chapters. The concepts related to organisational dynamics are described in the first two chapters. Chapter 1 presents the genesis of the book and explains how a new course on organisational dynamics led students to write real life cases about organisations and managers as a part of their learning pedagogy. The scope of organisational dynamics is defined and a framework for organisational analysis is proposed in the next chapter. Chapters 3 to 8 address different concepts of organisational dynamics. These modules have been drawn up on the basis of a host of issues pertaining to macro and micro level perspectives of an organisation. The main objective of these modules is to provide a framework for perspective building with regard to different aspects of organisational dynamics. A total of 33 cases have been presented along with a conceptual framework for each module.

Chapter 3 offers a framework of organisational dynamics as influenced by the internal and external environment of organisations and describes eight cases pertaining to the module. The cases presented cover issues such as organisational politics, games competitors play, malpractices, interdepartmental rivalry, organisational changes and internal work environment. They provide the reader an opportunity to analyse organisational dynamics from the perspective of the organisation and its environment—challenges posed by the internal and external environment and their impact on the organisation and its members.

The next chapter focuses on the influence of management practices on the functioning of an organisation. The two cases presented here deal with the dynamics at the top management level of an organisation. These cases demonstrate how pulls and pushes on account of power play cause organisation-wide conflict and how organisations respond to it and/or suffer from its consequences.

Chapter 5 discusses issues that managers experience when personal and social issues overlap with organisational boundaries. The nine cases presented here deal with issues such as personal ambitions, need for recognition, need for helping other employees, interpersonal conflicts and how these issues affect personal and social life.

The subsequent chapter proposes a conceptual framework for prospective managers to develop an organisational perspective that facilitates their integration into organisational realities. The six cases are based on the first encounter of new managers with organisational realities. The cases focus on issues of discrimination, disappointments, lackadaisical attitudes of colleagues and value dilemmas in adjusting to the organisational culture.

Chapter 7 on 'Mentoring and Empowerment' proposes a mechanism for mentoring and empowerment to organisations for effectively utilising the potential of its people in an environment of global competition and technological advances. The module includes four cases which discusses issues of development of individual potential, sacrifices and conflicts in the process of nurturing employees' potential.

The last chapter discusses a wide range of crisis situations that may disrupt the functioning of organisations. The three cases deal with the problem evolving the workers' union, issue of internal security and communal and political issues.

REFERENCES

Harvey, Michael and Buckley, M. Ronald. (2002). Assessing the 'conventional wisdoms' of management for the 21st century organization. *Organizational Dynamics*, *30*(4), 368–378.

Mintzberg, Henry and Gosling, Jonathan R. (2002, first quarter). Reality programming for MBAs. *Strategy+Business*, www.strategy-business.com.

Nevins, Mark David and Stumpf, Stephen A. (1999, third quarter). 21st century leadership: Redefining management education: Educating managers in the modern era. *Strategy+Business*, www.strategy-business.com.

Patel, V.G. and Jain, G.R. (1991). Reviewing curriculum in management for IIMs. Unpublished paper. *EDII*, Ahmedabad.

2

❖

emerging trends in
organisational dynamics

Expected Learning Outcomes

♦ *Identify factors that drive today's organisations to shift to a new paradigm of organisational fluidity and flexibility.*

♦ *Define flexible ODy in the current context of fluid organisational arrangements posing new challenges to managers.*

♦ *Comprehend the framework for a flexible ODy paradigm for analysing issues in organisational dynamics.*

CHANGING LANDSCAPE OF ORGANISATIONS

The UN Secretary-General Kofi Annan once told the UN General Assembly, 'The most important lesson of the 20th century was that centrally planned systems do not work'. He went on to explain that the world economies are transforming and, increasingly, political and economic decisions are being based on people's (beneficiaries') participation (Mike and Slocum Jr, 2003). This phenomenon seems to be equally relevant to the corporate world. Linearity and centralised decision-making systems are no longer relevant in the present-day's context where market trends are becoming increasingly complex and driven by breakthroughs in technology, new products and services, and new systems of delivering values to the stakeholders. These changes, in fact, are leading to the formation of new zones of intense economic and customer-centric activities (Becker, Huselid and Ulrich, 2001).

Andy Grove, chairman of Intel, wrote in his book *Only the Paranoid Survive*, 'all industries will eventually face significant changes in their competitive environments that will result from dramatic breakthroughs in new technologies, changes in customer demand, or the rise of new competitors' (James, 2003). The pressure on organisations is to continuously learn and rapidly adapt to the changing landscape of business and industry. Product life cycles have been shortened considerably. This trend is being observed even in the earlier 'staid' industries like automotive, medical equipment, electronic instruments and financial services (Butcher and Clarke, 2002; Lei and Slocum Jr, 2002). In order to emphasise the pace of changes (Lei and Slocum Jr, 2002), Grove used the term 'inflection point' (James, 2003) to characterise the nature of these profound and sudden changes in the environment that often spell a major crisis for firms and signify the potential for a radical transformation of an industry's structure.

Successful organisations can no longer gain competitive advantage merely through pricing strategies. What is required is constant innovation by way of introducing new products, services, brands and new management systems. Intangible assets are key success indicators in organisations because of their long-term sustainability. The traditional organisational systems of hierarchy, order and instructions are no longer adequate. Organisations are increasingly adopting networked enterprise systems, with a framework for integration of knowledge and empowerment of stakeholders. In order to sustain and grow in the face of an uncertain future, organisations are switching over to internal marketing dynamics in which internal units work as independent enterprises and even compete with each other in terms of quality, innovation, speed and cost (Halal, 1994; Lei and Slocum Jr, 2002). Virtual work groups and organisations, penetration of technology into management decision-making, and increased dependence on interorganisational relationships are the hallmark of present and future organisations (Harvey and Buckley, 2002; Johnson and Macy, 2001).

THE NEED FOR A NEW PARADIGM OF ORGANISATIONAL DYNAMICS

Classical organisation theories advocated largely structured approaches to dealing with the dynamics of managing people and performance. These theories were replete with principles or techniques of management such as span-of-control, line and staff differentiation, and chain-of-command and scalar chain of authority (Harvey and Buckley, 2002). Haapasalo and Kess (2001) observed that even contemporary management theories lead to systematic practices, which in fact limit the creative capacity of organisations. As a result of these theories the mechanism and results get priority over the process and content. One of the main assumptions of these theories is that organisations operate in a relatively stable environment and that it is predictable. While fluidity in organisational systems has become a reality, these theories largely advocate an open-and-closed system paradigm.

Classical and contemporary theories and practices in organisations have been considerably influenced by the Hawthorne experiments. In a series of experiments conducted between 1924 and 1933 at the Western Electric Company, Mayo and his associates (Epstein, 2003) concluded that employees worked harder if they believed that the management was concerned about their welfare and supervisors paid special attention to them. It was held that employees valued their membership in the group, and since the work had high performance norms, members' productivity continued to increase despite physically uncongenial surroundings. However, experiences of the 9/11 incident are in complete contrast to the Hawthorne studies. On 11 September 2001, two pilots, five flight attendants and 33 passengers responded to an unprecedented hijacking of a US aircraft. Mid-flight, in just about 30 minutes, a few passengers and the crew formed a team. They quickly talked through the situation, worked out a plan, and took the decision to divert the aircraft crash planned by the hijackers from a highly populated area to an isolated open field in Pennsylvania (Haapasalo and Kess, 2001; Kayes, 2003). This incident is a classic example of environmental turbulence/unexpected event from unknown sources affecting modern business corporations. The experience of 9/11 is becoming increasingly relevant to organisational reality. In the current environment, organisations cannot survive with a predetermined and structured road map for guiding and supporting the workforce as advocated by the classical and contemporary management theorists. Managers need to be empowered to work in a temporary organisational and team structure and can no longer depend upon an established hierarchical organisational system. These teams need to quickly respond to emerging opportunities or problems without having to wait for guidance or prescribed parameters for making decisions. The voluminous organisational manuals that guide managerial behaviour for interacting with the environment are becoming increasingly irrelevant and outdated.

To sum up, organisational theories encourage managers to be rational decision-makers and analyse information with functional expertise (Harvey and Buckley, 2002; Matson, Patiath and Shavers, 2003). Makridakis (1996) observed that 'the biggest challenge for firms will not be to follow the latest management theories or tools or imitate the strategies of the today's most successful companies but a fundamental understanding of the present and correct anticipation of forthcoming changes and their implications.' In the changing macro and micro environmental contexts of organisations, managers can no longer be expected to replicate organisational models offered by management gurus but have to think out of the box to create new approaches and methods for dealing with organisational dynamics.

ORGANISATIONAL DYNAMICS DEFINED

Contemporary Organisational dynamics as a process helps in analysing and dealing with what managers think about their own organisation with respect to how it works, its values, how it enables and/or inhibits their ability to carry out their work, how they respond when they see an opportunity or a problem, and how and which decisions to make to achieve the best possible result. These issues are important for building managers' capacity in handling organisational dynamics. Here ODy is a managerial capability that allows managers to go beyond the theories in creating organisational solutions in the face of internal and external environmental pressures.

The term 'Organisational Dynamics' (ODy) as used in the book refers to 'understanding the art and science of organisations, in which every member of the organisation responds to, and/or is subjected to, changes in the business landscape requiring unprogrammed and fluid adaptations (human, institutional, transformational and performance dynamics) for effective organisational solutions.' ODy would, therefore, essentially mean the extent to which an organisation empowers its managers to deal with internal and external dynamics through adaptations and rearrangement of its infrastructure. This approach to organisational dynamics is critical to organisations that are constantly being challenged by the unprecedented rate of change, extension of business operations in multicultural settings across the globe, complexity of business transactions, and sudden and unexpected events that disrupt the regular functioning of organisations.

The span of formulation and obsolescence of theories and models in ODy is becoming shorter on account of the rate of environmental changes; by the time these theories and models reach management schools for training future managers, they have probably become obsolete. It is therefore emphasised that learning about ODy should be largely through the enhancement of the capacity to analyse issues and challenges that organisations and managers experience and through the review of new approaches being evolved for dealing with challenges posed by the internal and external environment.

TRADITIONAL ODY PARADIGM

Traditional organisational models suggest that ODy comprises tangible parts such as structure, people, tasks and resources. These models also include some of the less tangible aspects of an organisation such as history, values, politics and leadership (Nadler and Tushman, 1977). Such models largely emphasise the relationship among different parts of an organisation (see Figure 2.1). These patterns of relationship assume that an organisation is made up of static patterns of relationship among its parts and intervention to modify these parts is largely through a systematic structuring of feedback.

The traditional ODy paradigm presumes that the environment is relatively stable and predictable. However, in the current context, organisations perceive the environment as unpredictable and turbulent and hence not a stable influence for the day-to-day decision-making process. This view is supported by an article in HBR (2003) which observed, 'given the continued economic uncertainty and loss of faith in corporate leaders, organisations are challenging assumptions about business, leadership, and people who make organisations work.'

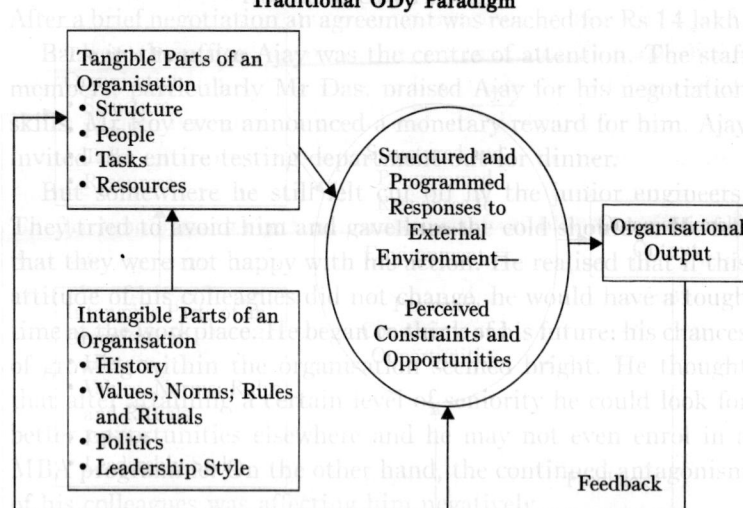

Figure 2.1
Traditional ODy Paradigm

For dealing with organisational dynamics in the light of the constantly changing environment, Bower (2003) argued that organisations with rigid organisational structure would not be able to respond to the challenges of globalisation and localisation and hence, proposed a framework of 'Velcro organisation' which allows managers to quickly rearrange roles and relationship to respond to the task.

THE NEED FOR A FLEXIBLE ODY PARADIGM

A flexible approach to an ODy paradigm is to facilitate managers to view the patterns of relationships across team or units as temporary and explore how these relationships can be restructured for effectively responding to external challenges. This approach to ODy helps organisations to not only leverage their capabilities creatively, but also enables them to quickly respond to sudden changes in the environment. Flexible ODy models are based on the rule of 'ground zero' where theories and practices are evolved based on what managers actually do in a particular situation and time rather than be guided by what they should do or what is normally done. A flexible ODy framework is explained in Table 2.1 by way of illustrating current issues in ODy and current drivers of a flexible ODy paradigm.

FRAMEWORK FOR ANALYSING ORGANISATIONAL DYNAMICS

The proposed model for analysing organisation dynamics is to enable organisations and managers to create organisational solutions in the face of internal and external environmental challenges. This framework is based on four components of organisational processes—human dynamics, institutional dynamics, transformational dynamics and performance dynamics. Each of these components is connected by an interactive mechanism. This mechanism enables the dynamics at any level in any of the components to trigger issues within any other component. For example, a decision to reduce costs on market development (performance dynamics) may increase stress perception or cause attrition among employees (human dynamics), reduce the market share (performance dynamics), and challenge the inadequacy of the structure or system in dealing with emerging issues (transformation). As these issues spread to cause an organisation-wide crisis, it may affect the dynamics at the governance level (institutional component).

The interactive framework for organisational dynamics is presented in Figure 2.2. It postulates the cause–effect relationship across the four components by proposing four interactive mechanisms. The institutional component of organisational processes shapes and reshapes human dynamics. This component, when empowered, can lead to dynamics at the institutional component of organisational processes. The latter governs the transformational dynamics for creating the organisational infrastructure for conducting day-to-day operations. The transformational component of organisational processes leads to dynamics at the performance level, which influences it back. The three components—human, transformational and performance—interact aggressively and cause dynamics throughout an organisation. The dynamics at the institutional level are relatively less aggressive and are caused in extreme situations such as a crisis.

Table 2.1
Framework for Flexible Organisational Dynamics

Current Issues in Organisations	Drivers of a Flexible Organisational Paradigm
• Spread of risk to reduce the likely effects of uncertainty due to changes in market and industry (Si and Bruton, 2003).	• Formation of organisational networks and multicultural team structure with competitors, suppliers and customers (Kayes, 2003).
• Non-linear thinking approach for dealing with unexpected events, new technologies, globalisation of economies, and spread of knowledge through internet (Glass, 1996; Kayes, 2003; Shrader and McConnell, 2002).	• Development of virtual teams and organisations, where employees may be spread across the globe, rather than be physically present in one office space, and can interact with key stakeholders through the use of network technologies such as e-teams (Becker et al., 2001; Harvey and Buckley, 2002; Zaccaro and Bader, 2003).
• Development of organisational strength in innovation that enables it to harmonise technology with the current and future needs of customers (Hutt and Walker, 1995; Mohrman, Finegold and Klein, 2002).	• Localisation of decision-making through empowerment of frontline managers and team structure (Butcher and Clarke, 2002).
• Growing emphasis on building intangible assets for long-term sustainability rather than focusing on narrow goals of financial profitability (Becker et al., 2001).	• Creation of an organisational system and culture of learning and unlearning for quick response to emerging challenges (Epstein, 2003; James, 2003).
• Organisational infrastructure needs be like Velcro, cohesive and workable when in place, but capable of being easily rearranged when circumstances and strategy call for it (Bowers, 2003).	• Automation of routine jobs leading to flattening of the chain of command. • Organisational hierarchy is being replaced by clusters of internal enterprises which work as independent companies and foster entrepreneurial synergy and collaboration within the corporate community (Halal, 1994).

The interactive mechanisms that allow the flow of energy to and from each component of organisational processes are personal and social dimensions interfacing with the organisation and its environment, corporate governance, empowerment and mentoring. These interactive mechanisms need to be constantly analysed by managers for dealing with organisational dynamics. Based on the cases presented in this book, a set of issues emerging under each component has been identified and presented in Figure 2.2 to illustrate the nature of issues that may emerge.

Figure 2.2
Interactive Framework for Organisational Dynamics

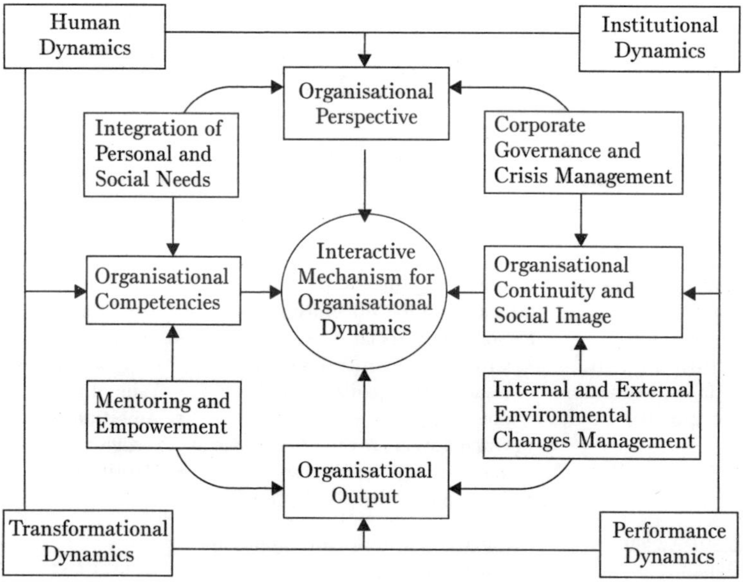

human dynamics

One of the key sources of dynamics is the stakeholders of an organisation. These stakeholders are people occupying different levels and roles within and outside the organisation. They may include employees, suppliers and customers. Human dynamics arise largely due to the variety of behavioural orientation of the stakeholders in terms of their needs, motives, attitudes, values, beliefs, educational levels, skills and family and cultural background. The interaction of these elements produces extreme level of dynamics in terms of pulls and pushes. The traditional organisational paradigm tends to control these dynamics through rigid organisational structures and practices while a flexible ODy approach uses these dynamics to leverage on the diverse capability of its stakeholders. The process helps in handling or responding to personal and social needs of people through a process of building organisational perspective. A set of issues such as stress, attrition, discrepancy, disappointment, value dilemmas, ambition, recognition and career growth that may be the cause of human dynamics or the effects of institutional, transformational and performance dynamics is presented in Table 2.2.

Table 2.2
Framework of Analysis of Organisational Dynamics

Components of Organisation Processes	Interactive Mechanism	Issues of Dynamics (Covered by Cases)
Human Dynamics Chemistry of motives, needs, attitudes, beliefs, social and education background.	Building Organisation Perspective (Mechanism for Integrating Personal and Social Needs) • Crossing of personal and social issues into organisational boundaries. • Organisation crossing into personal and social life of an employee. • Managerial identity development.	• Stress and attrition. • Discrepancy and disappointment. • Value dilemmas. • Ambition and recognition. • Career growth.
Institutional Dynamics Facilitator of flow of inputs and outputs centred on core of organisational culture, values, vision, mission, goals and policies.	Ensuring Continuity and Maintain Social Images of the Organisation (Mechanism of Corporate Governance and Organisational Crises Management) • Parameters of corporate governance for establishing good intentioned management. • Predicting future and anticipation of crises and prevention mechanism. • Recovery and renewal from crises.	• Ethical and unethical practices. • Media controversy. • Legal and gender challenges. • Political interferences.

Components of Organisation Processes	Interactive Mechanism	Issues of Dynamics (Covered by Cases)
Transformational Dynamics Operational competence development through the use of organisational infrastructure (enterprise) such as structure, systems, strategies and style.	Building Organisational Competencies (Mentoring and Empowerment Mechanism) • Motivation development. • Development and nurturance of talent. • Change management. • Team building.	• Internal work procedures and pressures. • Role ambiguity. • Change management. • Stiff targets. • Alignment with new demands.
Performance Dynamics Products, services, corporate image, feedback from customers, market share, growth of tangible and intangible assets.	Creating Organisational output for Sustainability (Mechanism for Managing Internal and External Environmental Changes) • Learning systems. • Tracking societal and industrial trends. • Alignment of internal processes. • Responding to new demands.	• Dealing with unstructured organisational set-up. • Roadblocks to delivery of services. • Performance versus mediocrity.

institutional dynamics

The institution is the core of any organisation which facilitates the flow of inputs and outputs around certain key values, and creates a culture for working toward its vision and mission. Stakeholders join the organisations with different sets of orientation which need to be harmonised according to the institutional dynamics. Similarly, stakeholders contribute to the further development of the organisation as an institution for meeting new challenges. The institutional framework of an organisation is represented by its governance system which is largely accountable for ensuring the survival of the organisation in the face of security risks. This component of organisational processes is about building organisational capacity for meeting current and future challenges. It, therefore, ensures that organisational resources are continuously created and invested for meeting its goal and makes possible arrangements in anticipation of and for prevention of likely security risks and also for organisational recovery from crises. A good intentioned management forms the institutional core of an organisation. The issues at this component level are change initiation, unethical practices, media controversy, legal and gender challenges, and other environmental issues such as social, political, or ecological conflict. These issues can lead to positive and/or negative effects throughout an organisation.

transformational dynamics

The transformation component of an organisation is responsible for making effective arrangement for operations through the mobilisation of resource inputs and delivery of output such as services to its stakeholders. This component comprises structure, strategies, systems and style. Transformational dynamics works as an enterprise and is responsible for obtaining results through the organisational infrastructure. Mentoring and empowerment are the twin processes of organisational transformation. They generate the required level of motivation and competence for effectively executing the activities of an organisation. The main transformational activities are development or nurturance of talent, team building and managing change to work towards the organisational mission. The possible issues that may arise here are internal work pressures, role ambiguity and setting up of difficult targets. Many of these issues are probably due to dynamics in the human, institutional and performance components.

performance dynamics

The performance of an organisation is the key to its sustainability. The elements at this level include products and services, corporate image, market share and growth of tangible and intangible assets. The dynamics at the level of organisational processes is extremely powerful as it is an indicator of the overall health of an organisation. The performance of an organisation is the outcome of the interaction of human, institutional and transformational processes; but this component in turn governs the dynamics among the other three. The internal–external environment interface makes performance dynamics an interactive process. The dynamics involve developing a learning mechanism, chaos approaches to changing trends, dealing with roadblocks to the delivery of services, dealing with an unstructured set-up and ambiguity in the needs and issues of stakeholders.

Summing up

An analysis of organisation dynamics is proposed as an approach for constantly learning about issues that managers experience while dealing with changes in the environment. Managers need to collect information about the four components of an organisation as depicted in Figure 2.2. The main sources of information on organisational dynamics are people and operations in the organisation. Managers may collect information using methods like observation, structured or unstructured interviews with employees and other stakeholders, conducting meetings, seeking feedback and views about various events, actions, performance results, and undertaking periodic formal or informal audit of systems and structures. The information collected may be used for examining the possible roots of issues, consequences of various situations, and drawing likely patterns of relationship between internal and external changes. The purpose of organisational analysis is not to identify particular individuals accountable for causing issues in the organisation but to enhance understanding of the causes and effects of dynamics as a learning process. Such an understanding will help manage fluidity in organisational systems and empower managers to deal with the dynamics effectively.

Cases in organisational dynamics pertaining to different components of an organisational system will introduce the reader to the nature of organisational dynamics and issues that managers experience in different contexts. These cases can serve as important materials for sensitising students and managers and enhancing understanding of the organisational perspective and system in relation to its different domains.

REFERENCES

Becker, E. Brian, Huselid, Mark A. and Ulrich, Dave. (2001). *The HR scorecard: Linking people, strategy, and performance.* Boston, MA: Harvard Business School Press.

Bower, Joseph L. (2003). Building the Velcro organization: Creating value through integration and maintaining organization-wide efficiency. *Ivey Business Journal*, November/December, 1–11.

Butcher, David and Clarke, Martin. (2002). Organizational politics: The cornerstone for organizational democracy. *Organizational Dynamics, 31*(1), 35–46.

Epstein, Edwin M. (2003). How to learn from the environment about the environment: A pre-requisite for organisational well-being. *Journal of General Management, 29*(1), 68–80.

Glass, Neil (1996). Chaos, nonlinear systems and day-to-day management. *European Management Journal, 14*(1), 98–106.

Haapasalo, Harri and Kess, Pekka. (2001). In search of organisational creativity: The role of knowledge management. *Creativity and Innovation Management, 10*(2), 110–118.

Halal, William E. (1994). From hierarchy to enterprise: Internal markets are the new foundation of management. *Academy of Management Executive, 8*(4), 69–83.

Harvey, Michael and Buckley, M. Ronald. (2002). Assessing the 'conventional wisdoms' of management for the 21st century organization. *Organizational Dynamics*, *30*(4), 368–378.

HBR. (2003). Breakthrough ideas for tomorrow's business agenda.

Hutt, Michael D. and Walker, Beth A. (1995). Hurdle the cross-functional barriers to strategic change. *MIT Sloan Management Review*, *36*(3), 22–30.

James, Constance R. (2003). Designing learning organizations. *Organizational Dynamics*, *32*(1), 46–61.

Johnson, Douglas B. and Macy, Granger. (2001). Using environmental paradigms to understand and change an organization's response to stakeholders. *Journal of Organizational Change Management*, *14*(4), 314–334.

Kayes, D. Christopher. (2003). Proximal team learning: Lesson from United Flight 93 on 9/11. *Organizational Dynamics*, *32*(1), 80–92.

Lei, David and Slocum Jr, John W. (2002). Organizational design to renew competitive advantages. *Organizational Dynamics*, *31*(1), 1–18.

Makridakis, Spyros. (1996). Factors affecting success in business: Management theories/tools versus predicting change. *European Management Journal*, *14*(1), 1–20.

Matson, Eric, Patiath, Pradip and Shavers, Tim. (2003). Stimulating knowledge sharing: Strengthening your organization's internal knowledge market. *Organizational Dynamics*, *32*(3), 275–285.

Mike, Barry and Slocum Jr, John W. (2003). Slice of reality: Changing culture at Pizza Hut and Yum! Brands, Inc. *Organizational Dynamics*, *32*(4), 319–330.

Mohrman, Susan A., Finegold, David and Klein, Janice A. (2002). Designing the knowledge enterprise: Beyond programs and tools. *Organizational Dynamics*, *31*(2), Autumn, 134–150.

Nadler, D. and Tushman, M. (1977). 'A Diagnostic Model for Organization Behaviour', in J.R. Hackman, E. Lawler and L. Porter (Eds), *Perspectives on behaviour in organizations*. New York: McGraw-Hill, pp. 85–100.

Shrader, Ralph W. and McConnell, Mike. (2002). Security and strategy in the age of Discontinuity: A management framework for the post-9/11 world. *Strategy+Business*, first quarter. (www.strategy+business.com).

Si, Steven X. and Bruton, Garry D. (2003). Beyond national boundaries: Considering the view from both sides of the table. *Organizational Dynamics*, *32*(4), 384–395.

Zaccaro, Stephen J. and Bader, Paige. (2003). E-leadership and challenges of leading e-teams: Minimizing the bad and maximizing the good. *Organizational Dynamics*, *31*(4), 377–387.

3

❖

organisation and its environment

Expected Learning Outcomes

♦ *Identify internal and external environmental pressure for organisational change.*

♦ *Critically evaluate approaches dealing with organisational dynamics in*
    closed or mechanistic model of organisation, and
    open or organic model of organisation.

♦ *Identify issues that managers experience in dealing with organisational dynamics caused by internal and external pressures.*

Organisations have to constantly respond to or deal with sudden changes and unexpected events that impact the landscape of the industry as well as the company. For example, SARS originated in China, but its effect spread across the world, causing huge economic losses to organisations and nations (Mike and Slocum Jr, 2003). The environment of an organisation is becoming increasingly volatile as it operates in multiple environmental settings. A major concern of organisations is how to evolve flexible organisational arrangements that enable them to deal with situations of crises, global competitiveness, total quality management, environmentalism and ethics (Mitroff and Mason, 1994). Whether willing or not, organisations have to develop their capabilities to respond to the pressures of changes in a technology-driven global economy and market (Krell, 2000). They have to constantly adapt and modify their internal work environment to creatively respond to the demands and changes in the internal and external environment (James, 2003).

ORGANISATIONAL APPROACHES TO ENVIRONMENTAL CHANGES

Organisations interact and deal with environmental changes depending upon their structural system. Some organisations are more internal need driven and create a rigid organisational structural system. These organisations are known as closed or mechanistic and tend be bureaucratic. Another set of organisations are driven largely by market or environmental need and are based on an organic or open organisational system. Such organisations tend to be flexible and adaptable. The organisational approaches in these two types of organisational systems respond differently to environmental changes. These approaches and the issues facing managers are discussed in the following.

closed or mechanistic organisational system

Organisations that are driven more by their internal need or internal work culture rather than external environmental demands are based on a closed or mechanistic model of organisational system. Their organisational culture is largely shaped by values, beliefs and attitudes held by the owner-managers or the top management team and implemented through well-defined organisational policies, procedures, roles and responsibilities (Lei and Slocum Jr, 2002). These organisations tend to follow a formal and bureaucratic system. Examples of such organisations include large corporations, government and, military establishments and family-managed enterprises.

The interaction of these organisations with the external environment is extremely limited. Organisational dynamics are largely determined by internal forces as in the short term these organisations remain largely unresponsive to external pressures (Matson, Patiath and Shavers, 2003). Change initiatives follow formal procedures and seek approval from the top management. Deviation from the formal rules or policies is normally avoided even if it is in the interest of the organisation. As a result, the speed of change in such organisations in the short term is extremely slow. However, managers do experience high levels of pressure to perform on account of external changes. Changes are initiated through a planned approach and the pace of introduction of change is relatively slow. The change initiative is often resisted by the internal stakeholders. For example, despite a clear trend of computerisation of business operations, many organisations such as nationalised banks, government corporations, judiciary systems, hospitals and railways took a long time to incorporate the new system. The internal organisational system often discourages managers to experiment with new and less known methods and techniques. Managers in these organisations find themselves in a tight spot as they are not empowered to make decisions to effectively respond to the demands of an unexpected situation.

open or organic organisational system

Organisations that are based on an open or organic organisational system empower their managers to actively interact with the external environment and continuously adopt new technologies or redesign internal processes and strategies. Such organisations respond effectively to conditions of uncertainty.

As changes in such organisations occur almost in a 'volatile' (continuous upheaval) manner, internal dynamics in these organisations are intense. Managers constantly adapt to and cope with external pressures. Further, they are equipped to adopt new management structures according to requirements, upgrade their capabilities with a new perspective of business and market, and develop skills for adopting new management practices in sync with the environment.

ISSUES IN ORGANISATIONAL DYNAMICS

Internal and external pressures do cause an intense level of organisational dynamics in both closed and open organisational set-ups. Managers may experience several issues while responding to changes in the environment.

1. Managers operating in a closed or mechanistic organisational setting tend to be more comfortable with traditional management practices based on a multidivisional or specialised functional structure. They tend to predict the environment based on past trends and use long-term strategic corporate planning to respond to environmental challenges (Khandwalla, 1977). In the event of sudden changes, they use a 'quick-fix approach' by way of making minor structural or policy changes leading to cost reduction or minimisation of immediate negative effects (Mitroff and Mason, 1994). However, these changes are ad hoc and do not transform or change their fundamental belief about the process of management. As a result, the organisation is not able to secure full advantage of the change. Managers in such an organisation develop a sense of inadequacy in responding to environmental issues and feel uncertain about the future

of their organisation in the context of the rapidly changing business scenario.

2. In the current context, organisations have to constantly formulate strategies and organisational arrangements with for more focus on time and market (Lei and Slocum Jr, 2002). For example, an organisation may suddenly find restrictions imposed on its business activities due to the actions of consumer associations or changes in government policy or amendment in the legal system of a nation. In such environmental conditions, managers may feel caught up as they perceive the need to shift to a new paradigm of organisational management practices. The organisation will have to undertake massive restructuring exercises in order to align itself with internal and external demands. The transition and adjustment phase of the organisational change process creates a new set of dynamics among managers (Matson, Patiath and Shavers, 2003). Managers may feel unsure of their future roles in the organisation or experience conflict with the new work environment or pressure for developing a new set of skills (Hill and Stephens, 2003).

3. Managers have to change their pattern of thinking and relationship with other organisational units, which may affect their psychological and emotional state. For example, they have to constantly unlearn and learn new management methods for decision-making because of rapid environmental changes (Kast and Rosenzweig, 1985). These changes may instil a sense of insecurity in some of them, while others may be able to transform these changes into a new set of opportunities. Some managers may effectively cope with these changes, while others may feel stressed out. The negative effects of environmental changes occur largely when the organisational arrangements are relatively rigid. The issues of dealing with organisational dynamics may become serious when managers refuse to accept that changes in the internal and external environment produce a new set of organisational dynamics.

4. Managers have to continuously work with environmental transitions and, hence, they need to overcome a rigid mindset and shift to new paradigms of managing. They need to continually review their inter- and intra-organisational relationships. Some managers may adopt a new perspective while others may continue to cling to past practices. Those who cannot unlearn or switch to new learning may try to suppress others from looking forward progressively to future challenges and thinking as per the new paradigm. The absence of this culture of learning and unlearning causes conflicts among organisational members and work units in the process of adapting to new methods of managment.

5. Managers have to continually break and consolidate new organisational shapes when needed. They have to invest in evolving new methods and techniques of organisational decision-making and not necessarily rely on popular organisational or management models. In this, organisations set an example by relying on the vision rather than looking into past precedence while evaluating a new plan or strategy. Staunch upholders of established norms may continue to oppose or challenge the innovative efforts of other managers. The outcome may be an increase in internal conflicts and the generation of 'pull and push' factors.

In the current situation, forces in the internal and external environment rarely follow past trends. The expected attitude is to shift from a linear thinking model to a chaos management model (Glass, 1996). This entails the capacity to think out of the box and create new methods and processes for managing organisational dynamics. To function in the changing environment, managers are continuously evolving new patterns of organisational relationships by accepting the flexibility of organisational arrangements. For this, managers may adopt a new form of organisational structure (such as a matrix structure or a virtual work group) that ensures greater organisational fluidity (Harvey and Buckley, 2002). Halal (1994) suggested internal marketing based enterprise structure as opposed to a hierarchical organisational system. Bower (2003) proposed a Velcro-like organisational system for quickly adapting to the changing circumstances.

CASES ON ORGANISATIONAL DYNAMICS

Nine cases on 'Organisation and its environment' have been presented here. The cases reveal how the emerging social, economic, technological global market system affects organisational dynamics with a great degree of variation. In some cases organisations could foresee the new pattern of changes and adapted to the new organisational systems, while in other cases they responded slowly or reactively. Each case sheds light on the dilemmas of managers who were proactively sensitive to internal and external dynamics and discusses how they introduced new methods of marketing or improved support systems in the light of a rigid organisational culture or structure. These cases have been grouped into two categories: internal work environment and external environmental changes.

internal work environment

Six cases focus on issues of organisational dynamics largely arising from the pull and push factors in the internal work environment. These cases cover a host of issues pertaining to internal work systems, culture, climate and the style of top management in different types of business operations—software production, call centre activities and industrial equipment designing.

'Sycophantic Colleagues' describe a young manager who, on joining a production house, found an unstructured organisational set-up and each of clarity in job profiling. The unstructured set-up created roadblocks for him in delivering quality output. He confronted the top management for streamlining the organisational systems. However, rather than improving the situation, this put him out of favour with the management.

'Modi Fire Protection Systems Pvt. Ltd' discusses a series of HR initiatives to improve organisational capabilities. The employees resisted these initiatives as they felt that these changes were inconsistent with the needs of the current management system which was characterised by weak support facilities, prejudices and favouritism. They harboured resentment toward the HR consultant because of his style and approach to their issues.

'Kaze Services—the Dilemma Prevails' focuses on a call centre where the employees engaged in unethical practices in order to meet the stringent service standards linked to performance evaluation.

'A Dream Shattered' describes the case of a manager who joined the organisation while it was in transition, changing its operating style from a typical privately held to a professional corporate culture. Despite this, many senior managers did not change their attitude. Though this new manager was recruited to initiate the new management system, the senior managers continued to engage him in routine jobs and did not allow him utilise his skills.

'A Success out of Failures' is about the launch of a new product by a pharmaceutical company which caused a ripple in the internal dynamics of the company. For proper management of the launch, a new team was formed comprising individuals from different levels of the company. The company soon experienced a cash crunch as the product was not moving and the stock piled up with dealers. Investigations revealed that the company's insider had played a game that had led to the disaster. The case discusses the measures taken by the company to emerge from this mess.

The BPO sector is explored in 'Tanya's Dilemma'. As the organisation handled a diverse set of clients, the work environment was vibrant and competitive. The emphasis was on the quality of work, with incentives for star employees. Employee burnout was high due to work pressure and competition. This resulted in high attrition levels. After assessing the situation, the team leader proposed reducing the workload and working at improving employee morale. However, not only did the senior manager reject all her recommendations, but also asked her to terminate the services of an employee with high potential because of his poor performance.

external environmental changes

Three cases focus on organisational sensitivity to external environmental pressures and changes and the capability of these organisations to respond by way of switching to more progressive management practices. The cases highlight how external environment changes impact internal organisational dynamics in four different industrial settings—car manufacturing, pharmaceuticals, software and financial services.

'Blaze Motor Corporation' discusses age-old selling techniques adopted during Diwali to sell more cars without taking into consideration actual purchase behaviour. However, the customers were not willing to buy a car even at a discounted rate because the company had resorted to cost leadership as a weapon for marketing and had completely ignored product innovation. When the marketing manager realised this, he called off the discount scheme at the cost of going against company practices.

'Future of a Brilliant Manager' describes a company in the financial sector. The company planned for a new service that required huge investments in new technology. The marketing manager and his team developed an innovative mechanism that was aimed to save on the investment costs. The product was launched, but did not do very well in the market. In the meantime the new CEO asked the team for a review report. He made it clear that in the light of the poor performance, withdrawing the service was a likely option.

'Difficult Transitions' focuses on a software company that made a transition to new technology following 9/11. A young manager proposed the use of Linux instead of Microsoft. A senior colleague opposed the proposal. A series of such confrontations frustrated the young manager who saw no future for himself in the organisation and considered resigning.

REFERENCES

Bower, Joseph L. (2003). Building the Velcro organization: Creating value through integration and maintaining organization-wide efficiency. *Ivey Business Journal*, November/December, 1–11.

Glass, Neil. (1996). Chaos, nonlinear systems and day-to-day management. *European Management Journal*, *14*(1), 98–106.

Halal, William E. (1994). From hierarchy to enterprise: Internal markets are the new foundation of management. *Academy of Management Executive*, *8*(4), 69–83.

Harvey, Michael, and Buckley, M. Ronald. (2002). Assessing the 'conventional wisdoms' of management for the 21st century organization. *Organizational Dynamics*, *30*(4), 368–378.

Hill, Ronald Paul and Stephens, Debra Lynn. (2003). The compassionate organization in the 21st century. *Organizational Dynamics*, *32*(4), 331–341.

James, Constance R. (2003). Designing learning organizations. *Organizational Dynamics*, *32*(1), 46–61.

Kast, Fremont E. and Rosenzweig, James. (1985). *Organization and management*, (4th edn). New York: McGraw-Hill.

Khandwalla, Pradip N. (1977). *The design of organizations*. New York: Harcourt Brace Jovanovich, Inc.

Krell, Terence C. (2000). Organisational longevity and technological change. *Journal of Organizational Change Management*, *13*(1), 8–13.

Lei, David and Slocum Jr, John W. (2002). Organizational design to renew competitive advantages. *Organizational Dynamics*, *31*(1), 1–18.

Matson, Eric, Patiath, Pradip and Shavers, Tim. (2003). Stimulating knowledge sharing: Strengthening your organization's internal knowledge market. *Organizational Dynamics*, *32*(3), 275–285.

Mike, Barry, and Slocum Jr, John W. (2003). Slice of reality: Changing culture at Pizza Hut and Yum! Brands, Inc. *Organizational Dynamics*, *32*(4), 319–330.

Mitroff, Ian I. and Mason, Richard O. (1994). Radical surgery: What will tomorrow's organizations look like? *Academy of Management Executive*, *8*(2), 11–21.

CASES ON ORGANISATION AND ITS ENVIRONMENT

key learnings

♦ *Identify a pertinent yet less discussed managerial skill in the modern day—managing your boss.*

♦ *Analyse the dynamics of change initiative which results in employees' disinterest and inefficiency.*

♦ *Identify challenges of change in a hierarchical organisational system.*

♦ *Experience the response of top management in handling dissent.*

♦ *Analyse the experience of managers when they face the 'everything is fair' syndrome in organisations.*

SYCOPHANTIC COLLEAGUES*

Som Dutt is a 25 year old professional working in ITV Pvt. Ltd, a production house based in Kolkata. After graduating in economics from Calcutta University, he obtained a diploma in mass communication from a reputed institute in Kolkata. He was awarded the ITA gold medal for journalism. He was selected by ITV during campus recruitment.

After working for just 4 months at ITV, he came to know that the company was being dissolved because of some internal issues. He applied to a reputed production house, Pan India Media Network, a Bombay-based television software production house. The company was involved in generating news and current affairs content for Indian and international channels. It was a medium-sized production house run by an entrepreneur, Mr Parmeet Sodhi. Some of the programmes and news bulletins produced by the company had received good media reviews. As a result Pan India had earned for itself a positive reputation in the market.

job profile

After an intensive recruitment process involving several rounds of interviews, Som was selected for the post of a correspondent. His job profile included reporting news events and filing spot and feature stories. He had to travel extensively for his stories and important news items.

Soon he had a good grip on his job, the working of the organisation, his duties and responsibilities. The work was challenging and he enjoyed it. Som realised that the organisational set-up was unstructured and roles were not clearly defined. Instead of being dissuaded, he took it as an opportunity to learn his job from different perspectives. The fluidity of the system gave him the space

*Acknowledgements: Noopur Keswani, Rohitash Srivastava, Sriya Narayan, Swati Ashok Garodia and Yamini Singh.

to work on several beats that would have come his way only after several years in a regular media house. He believed that this exposure at an early stage would help him enhance his skills.

Som noticed a few anomalies, such as, the attrition level was extremely high. Most of the staff switched jobs within 6 to 10 months and new people filled those positions. When he informally questioned his boss about this trend, he was told that their organisation worked as a family and issues like these were too trivial to be taken seriously.

moving up

His commitment to work and willingness to learn impressed his seniors. His first raise came within 2 months of his joining the organisation. He was given important assignments and handled key programmes produced by the company. Nine months later he was promoted to the post of a producer. He was entrusted the responsibility of managing the production of an important daily news bulletin, 'Asian Newstrack'.

His performance remained consistently high. Soon Som was considered a key member of the organisation. He enjoyed close relations with his seniors and was one of the most trusted staff members. Personally, he was satisfied with his job. The disorganised structure enabled him to experiment and try many things. His talent was recognised and he learnt a lot.

As Asian Newstrack was one of the most important news bulletins produced by the organisation, Som was supported by a 10-member team of the best reporters, cameramen and editors in the company. He was also in charge of editing the news bulletin and responsible for assigning spot stories and reports to his team of correspondents. With increased work pressure and responsibility, his job became more and more demanding. Gradually, he began to face problems of cooperation from the staff members. The very lack of structure that had helped him now affected the coordination and efficiency required in a demanding project like his.

lack of co-ordination

At times his camera team would be sent with other correspondents without his knowledge. Time and again, when his team needed a car to cover an important story, none would be available because someone else would have taken the vehicle. Som's colleagues often occupied the editing suite even during the slots allotted to him. Maintaining strict deadlines was necessary for Som as his programme was a daily news bulletin. Despite this, resources were often haphazardly allocated without any prioritisation. Weekly programmes were allotted to the camera team and the editing suite without consideration for the daily news items.

The task of ensuring that all the projects ran smoothly was entrusted to two coordinators who were appointed for the purpose. They were responsible for keeping a tab on news events across the country and arranging for the logistics of tape delivery by air, train, or other means. Som often felt that they tried to sabotage his work by not cooperating with him. After a while he realised that some of his colleagues were unhappy with his promotion and the consequent salary increase. The coordinators often ignored his requirements or did not provide him with resources in time. Som recalled one such incident.

His team was working on a significant news story for which it had to cover the speech of an eminent foreign delegate. The tapes of the event were to arrive by the 5 p.m. flight. The show was to go on air soon and the tapes had not yet arrived. Som asked the coordinator several times about the tapes. Each time he was told that they had not been delivered and he would be informed once they were delivered. At 6 p.m. he got the same answer. Finally around 7 p.m., he approached his senior and informed him that they would have to air the programme without video coverage as the tapes had not been delivered. His boss called up the coordinator to enquire about the tapes. To Som's astonishment the coordinator informed him that the tapes had been lying with him for 2 hours but no one had come to collect them. He felt like a fool before his boss.

valuable employee

Similar problems continued even after this episode. Som realised that the main reason for this was the lack of proper management in the organisation. His frequent promotions and salary inceases was causing discontent among many of his peers. The structure of remuneration differed even at the same level of hierarchy. Perks and incentives were given according to the whims and fancies of the owners of the organisation. Rewards were based on the proximity of the employee to his senior and not on realistic performance barometers. Improper structure, planning and control demanded that the employee had to manipulate things for getting his work done in time.

In the meantime Asian Newstrack got noticed by many other news agencies and production houses. Since the field was small, Som became well known in industry circles. He began to receive offers from various organisations that promised a higher designation and attractive remuneration. One such offer was from STN Productions, a large and well-known production house. The news of this offer reached the owners of Pan India before Som heard about it. He was called in by his seniors to discuss the issue.

He was welcomed affably by his seniors. They told him that they had come to know Som was unhappy in the company and was planning to leave and join STN. Som was surprised at the news of any such offer having been made. He averred that the pay had never been an issue for him. He was told,

> Every employee in this organisation is like a family member. You are one of our most valuable employees and we want you continue with us. We understand that in the past you have had some difficulties in delivering your work. But we also feel that we should acknowledge your contribution to the organisation. Hence, the Board has decided to give you a hundred percent hike in salary. We can also consider a zero percent interest car loan and a raise in your perks.

Som thought that this was the right opportunity to bargain with the management. He was in a position of advantage from where he could negotiate with the bosses to make some necessary changes in the organisational structure. He said that he would think about the offer and let them know his decision in a week's time. He did some groundwork before the next meeting. He told the management that giving him a raise was not as important as streamlining the operations. He made some suggestions to the top management as a part of the process of negotiation.

1. Stagger shifts for work in the editing suite, use of camera and machines and ensure optimal resource utilisation.
2. Put up a bulletin board for notification of delivery of new tapes.
3. Solve the problem of conveyance. As soon as a team reaches the venue it should relieve the car and not keep it.
4. Have a performance-based appraisal system.
5. Maintain a uniform salary slab for similar hierarchical levels and be transparent in the criteria used for giving perks and incentives.
6. Prioritise work in accordance with the deadlines to be met. Daily bulletins require priority over weeklies.

The management listened silently to his suggestions before asking him to meet the Board after a week.

no increment

Som was called again after five days and was told,

> Mr Dutt, we have seriously thought over your proposals and are ready to incorporate your suggestions. But now the management does not find itself in a position to give you an increment. We also cannot provide you with the interest-free car loan. If we give you a raise, others will start raising similar demands and we cannot afford to do this every time a problem comes up.

He was informed that the bosses had enough information to prove that Som was trying to influence the staff against the management. He was accused of being a unionist and a Leftist. He was warned to refrain from such activities or the management would consider disciplinary action against him. Som quietly returned to his table and sat in silence thinking. He interpreted the interaction as a clear indication that the management no longer wanted him around. He was disappointed. An hour later he submitted his resignation.

MODI FIRE PROTECTION SYSTEMS PVT. LTD*

Mr Patel, an alumnus of a leading business school in Mumbai, had worked as a HR manager for 4 years in two major FMCG companies and in a prominent construction company for 3 years. He is now a HR consultant to three companies in Ahmedabad, including Modi Fire Protection Systems Pvt. Ltd (MFPS).

MFPS, a Rs 6.85 crore enterprise, was founded in 1979 and has vast experience in designing and installing fire detection and fire protection systems. Its clients include public sector units and major industrial plants. Its headquarters are in Ahmedabad, with branch offices in Delhi and Mumbai. The Ahmedabad office is housed on two floors, in the basement as well as on the sixth floor.

objective appraisal

Mr Patel visited MFPS thrice a week. He put in a lot of effort to develop the company's employment policy. Job profiles were clearly defined. An objective appraisal system was put in place under which promotions were based on a judicious consideration of merit and seniority. Training programmes for technological enhancement and development of communication skills were organised. His current attempts were to involve the employees in the decision-making process. He encouraged them to drop their feedback on

*Acknowledgements: Noopur Keswani, Rohitash Srivastava, Sriya Narayana, Swati Ashok Garodia and Yamini Singh.

organisational functioning in a suggestion box set up for the purpose. The company had announced a monthly reward of Rs 1,000 for the best suggestion. He conducted regular staff meetings to apprise them of the prevalent rules and codes of conduct. The employers were happy with Mr Patel's initiatives.

However, there was discontent amongst the staff. Despite his best efforts, he noticed a general disinterest in his initiatives. Rumours of dissatisfaction with the appraisal system, poor enrolment in the managerial training programmes, failure of the suggestion box to elicit enthusiastic responses, and poor or no contribution from employees in the staff meetings were just some of the issues that concerned him.

The general manager, Mr Raikar, was happy with the well-defined job descriptions and saw good growth prospects for himself. However, he complained that even though employees were asked to evaluate themselves, the senior management had the last word regarding promotions. Favouritism and prejudice affected their judgement. He also objected to Mr Patel's interfering nature.

training programmes

Mr Bajaj, manager (contracts), saw no value add in attending the training programmes. For example, he did not understand why sales people were asked to attend computer workshops when most of them did not use computers at work. He was not enthusiastic about giving suggestions as he feared that he would be given the responsibility of implementing his ideas. He was confused about what constitutes latecoming and disliked confrontations about it at meetings. Mr Singhal, manager (accounts), had worked in MFPS for 15 years. He welcomed the automation and training programmes but was unhappy that his contribution to the organisation had neither been acknowledged nor monetarily rewarded. He was dissatisfied with the fact that informal gatherings were few and far between. He disliked the bureaucracy inherent in the system and the wastage of time, money and resources that it entailed.

Mr Singh, manager (purchase), had joined MFPS 6 months ago. He was overworked and irked by the fact that salaries were not paid regularly. Like Mr Singhal, he also believed that more financial incentives were in order. He thought his work was disorganised because often he had to report to two people simultaneously. Mr Garimella, manager (engineering), believed that all his activities were scrutinised by the HR consultant. He resented Mr Patel's attitude towards the employees of trying to coerce them into following organisational rules and working more effectively. He was, however, content with the level of interpersonal relationships at work.

slow and inefficient

When things began to get out of hand, Mr Patel thought it best to address the employees directly. On the issue of employee tardiness and apathy, Mr Patel confronted Mr Singh on his frequent latecoming. Mr Singh retorted that punctuality would not be an issue if employees were provided with office conveyance for daily commutation. He pointed out that he had made this suggestion 3 months ago but nothing had come out of it. Similarly, when Mr patel raised the issue of slow and inefficient inter-departmental communication with Mr Bajaj, the latter told him that as the two offices were separated by five floors, sending messages across was consuming time. Besides, the office space was insufficient and he often felt claustrophobic. Mr Garimella added that providing computer terminals and office mail IDs would greatly improve efficiency. He also made a request for a telephone allowance and cell phones for the managerial staff. The managers concurred that they wanted a HR consultant who was more approachable. They suggested the recruitment of a full-time HR manager who would better understand the organisational structure and functioning and be around when the need arose.

KAZE SERVICES—THE DILEMMA PREVAILS*

Kaze Services, a privately owned and operated company, was established in New York over 20 years ago. Over the years it has developed from an after-hours answering service into a fully integrated call centre. It now operates 24 hours a day, seven days a week and provides a wide range of telecommunication servicing options to various clients all over the world.

beyond the call of duty

Kaze Services is a single source integrated telephone service provider to corporate clients worldwide. The services include:

- Inbound customer services.
- Outbound tele-servicing.
- Website telephone support.
- Maintaining prime customer contact for utility companies.
- Providing solutions for a retail business.

Its client list encompasses all industry segments—banks, educational institutions, city councils, utility companies, manufacturers, distributors, help desks, meteorological information providers, national and international charities, direct response companies and insurance companies.

The company's profits worldwide increased from $63 million in 1987 to $287 million in 2003, that is, in a span of 16 years. It has been an industry leader for the past 15 years. Kaze Services' biggest asset is its highly motivated team, many of whom have been with the company for years. Mr Rowan Parkinson, president of Kaze Services once commented:

> We've developed a culture of customer focus that has ensured the organisation's success. That culture ensures that the customer

*Acknowledgements: Gautam Jain and Mohammad Ahmad.

care executives are managing more than just a phone call. They are managing a relationship between the client and their customers. Accordingly, our mission is to deliver quality service that consistently enhances our customer's service to their customers.

The motto of Kaze Services aptly reflects this objective—Beyond the call—that is, understanding customers' needs and providing them the best solutions and services.

Kaze Services in India

The company hierarchy is arranged in bands. At the bottom is a group of process associates governed by senior customer care executives. Above them are process developers. These three ranks form Band 5 of the company. Band 4 comprises assistant managers, managers and senior managers. The next band includes the operations leader of process and the assistant vice president. The vice president of process forms Band 2, and Band 1 comprises the CEO of the company in India.

In 1997 the company shifted its operations to India, though the head office was still located in New York. The reason for the shift was that the operating costs in India were eight times lower than in the US. Further, increased competition in the US market was squeezing the company's margins. When Kaze shifted to India, it made sure that the customer satisfaction level did not decline and the standards of service for which it was globally recognised were maintained.

Lifesavers Medical Equipment (LME), a producer of medical equipment, was a major client of Kaze. Since it was a significant revenue earner, Kaze had a separate department of 45 executives to handle the account. All calls of LME were handled from India. Across America, LME had contracts with various hospitals and medical institutions to which it supplied medical equipment and provided after-sales service. It had field engineers who went on-site and serviced faulty medical equipment. For instance, if an X-ray machine or a CT scanner was not working, the customer (hospital) would contact the Kaze Services call centre in India on a toll free number and describe the problem. The executive at the call centre would then page the respective field engineer for that area in America. After receiving the necessary details the engineer would visit the site for servicing. If the hospital did not have a service contract with Lifesavers but required the service then Kaze Services billed the hospital for the service provided. The Kaze billing department was set up for transferring the additional business to LME.

customer care

Customer satisfaction was the primary objective of Kaze. For this purpose, meeting response targets was one of the company policies. Sometimes the executives would get a call from a hospital with a patient on the operating table and thus it was all the more important to maintain efficiency of service.

When Kaze was based in the US it had certain locational advantages. Being a local call centre meant that it could function more methodically and was customer centric. When it shifted to India it had some 20 odd employees in the department. Driven by customer demand, the size of the department grew to 45 employees. Customer care executives handled the calls. Managers and senior managers were responsible for maintaining deadlines and achieving project targets. The guideline was to complete a call within 160 seconds. If a call exceeded the allotted time the executive had to make up for it by reducing the time on another call. Also, he was not supposed to put the customer on hold for more than 16 seconds. The answer rate for calls had to be a minimum of 97 per cent; that is, of all the calls that came through the medical system, at least 97 of them had to be answered. If a customer disconnected the call before it was answered it was considered an unanswered call. These targets were sacrosanct because of the importance attached by the company to customer satisfaction. If employees failed to meet these criteria thrice consecutively, they were dismissed. Warning letters were issued for each lapse.

unethical practices

Since the consequences were so dire, employees sometimes com-promised on company values and individual ethics. They developed their own innovative ways to beat the system. If a call exceeded its time limit or the answer rate dropped to less than 97 per cent or both happened, senior executives would make calls from their respective work stations to the Kaze medical system. As soon as the agent attended the call, they would disconnect the line. This reduced the average call time and thus, on paper time limits were met. Similarly, the answer rates could also be artificially propped up. For instance, if in one day the medical system received 180 calls and only 174 calls were attended, the answer rate would be 96.66 per cent, that is, below the target level of 97 per cent. The senior executive would himself make 21 calls to the system raising the answer rate to 97.01 per cent, that is, 195 calls out of 201. Suppose the medical system's call centre received 250 calls with an average talk time of 162 seconds (2 minutes 42 seconds), the executives would make two calls for, say, 2 seconds each. Hence, the overall talk time would decline to 155.84 seconds, well within the limit of 160 seconds! The company had not installed any specific system to track these internal calls. Calls made by execu-tives were not monitored and hence could not be tackled.

In the US, Saturdays and Sundays are weekly holidays. Though this was not possible in the medical profession, the work volume was relatively less for Kaze over the weekends. A typical problem that arose when one of the few calls that came exceeded the stand-ard time limit, for example, it could increase dramatically to 15 minutes. The dilemma the executive faced was whether to discon-nect the line and displease the customer or continue with the call and risk a letter of warning. Sometimes a customer called up and then disconnected the line before being answered, not because there was a delay but perhaps there was an interruption from his side. For the call centre this counted as an unanswered call. In such instances, too, the executives resorted to the questionable method of internal calling.

Should the meeting of targets be given so much importance as was being done at Kaze medical system? Should meeting targets be at the cost of customer satisfaction? These were questions that troubled some people when executives tricked the company's management. These concerns came to a head when three executives were caught making these calls by the higher authorities. These executives were outstanding performers, who worked hard whenever the company needed them. When questioned, they said that, if they had not done this they would have been thrown out of the company, even though they were high performers. They kept the customer happy and went out of the way to help them. That was why their performance was also noticed.

The top management was in a dilemma as to what should be done with these executives. Should they be thrown out of the company or should they be retained? Each one was a star performer, the best in their respective teams.

A DREAM SHATTERED*

The weekend ended on a high note with a party. It was the birthday celebration of Rohan, Abhay's best friend. They had met after very long and had a great time together. After college, they had joined different organisations and had found it difficult to spend time together. 'But this is life', thought Abhay. The earlier one adapts to it the better. He felt morose as he climbed the stairs to his house and thought of having to go to office the next day.

phenomenal growth

Abhay was an engineering graduate who worked for Auto Equipments Pvt. Ltd, an export-oriented motor parts manufacturing

*Acknowledgements: Abir Kanjilal, Arvind Krishnan, Indranil Das, Nitin Kumar, Ratnakar Mani and Suman Nag.

unit. The organisation had seen rapid growth in the recent past and had a sizeable workforce. Its annual turnover was Rs 50 crore. It also produced automobile accessories for domestic customers. The company was setting up a state-of-the-art ERP-based plant in one of the biggest export processing zones near Delhi. However, it was not always easy for the company to meet deadlines.

The vice president, Sanjay Chug, and the personnel manager had interviewed Abhay at the time of recruitment. He was appointed an assistant engineer in the production planning and control department (PPC) of the company. He reported to the PPC manager, Ashwin. He had been told that the PPC manager was one of the oldest employees of the company and his experience was very important for the efficient functioning of the production department.

The culture of the company was undergoing a change from a traditional family-owned business to a MNC style of functioning. The new generation of owners was professionally qualified and aware of the need to replace obsolete practices with modern technology and transparency of operation. The customers were also looking for modernisation of processes. This could be possible only through a concurrent change in employees' outlook.

interaction with clients

Ashwin had seen the company evolve from a small firm to an efficient, medium-sized organisation. He had a thorough knowledge of the processes involved in production, the working and dealings with other departments as well as the company–client interaction patterns. On his first day at work Abhay had been puzzled by Ashwin's behaviour. Being a fresh graduate he had expected some formal training. Instead, the manager told him that, since the PCC department had to coordinate more with the purchase department he should sit in the purchase department to ease the process. He added that he would call Abhay whenever the need arose.

However, Abhay was rarely called as the manager continued to work with his old assistants. Abhay was without any work. With no formal on-the-job training and no contact with the everyday functioning of the PCC department, he felt he was intentionally being cut off from the main work. But the assistants could not have functioned without him. He was the engineer and no one else could have done his job. After talking to some other employees in the organisation he learnt that such problems were routine in the PCC department. This forced him to approach the VP with his problem.

He narrated the entire episode to the VP. After listening to him the VP informed him that engineers even in the past had faced similar problems with Ashwin. The organisation was shifting towards a corporate culture and some of the older employees were unable to adjust to the change from the earlier bureaucratic system. Though Ashwin was an asset to the organisation, he found the process of change very difficult. The VP wanted Abhay to co-operate with the manager and earn his faith, so as to be able to facilitate the process of change.

intentions backfire

Mr Chug summoned the clerks and assistants of the PPC department and instructed them to report to Abhay. The latter, in turn, was asked to submit summary reports to Ashwin. Arrangements were also made for Abhay to sit in his own department. But Ashwin neither looked at the summary reports nor called Abhay for any clarification. He also asked the clerks to continue to submit reports to him and functioned as he had earlier. A week later Abhay again met Mr Chug. His disappointment was growing. Out of sheer frustration Abhay asked his senior why they had recruited him if there was no need for an engineer in the PCC department. Understanding his dilemma Mr Chug entrusted him the task of creating a database of all the products the company had been manufacturing.

Soon Ashwin learnt that Abhay had bypassed him. He also came to know that Abhay had got an assignment from Mr Chug himself and had shown excellent results. He could not come to terms with the fact that the organisation was trying to 'push' a newcomer in his department. He began to call Abhay and assigned him work.

no relevance

Ashwin began to allot work to Abhay that the latter thought had no relevance. Abhay stayed back late to successfully complete the work given by both the PCC manager and the VC. Earlier the manager was the last person to leave the office whenever a container had to be dispatched. He now asked Abhay to stay on and handle the process. Abhay, however, despised this work as he thought that it did not call for any intellectual involvement and even a worker could do it.

Abhay had passed out from college with many dreams; the reality was nowhere close. He was not learning anything and the work was not contributing to his career. He was a mere cog in the wheel for the organisation and there seemed no reason for him to continue there.

A SUCCESS OUT OF FAILURES*

company background

Zala Pvt. Ltd, a well-known name in the pharmaceutical industry, has a product mix of Caramom, Zolox, Zipla and the market conqueror Zompez. Though all its products were doing well in the

*Acknowledgements: Atul Rohan Garg, Deepak Singh, Garima Gupta, Rashmi Wadhwa and Traptika Chauhan.

market, the company needed to go in for an expansion, as it had been long since it had done something innovative, which is necessary for any company to survive and remain in business. The pressure of consumer expectations was also a major factor for the company to take this decision.

the new product

The company decided to set up a herbal division. This division was expected to launch a few herbal products, since there was a high demand for such products in the market. Though the players in this industry were well established and well known, there were some who posed a stiff competition to Zala's planned line of herbal products. Some of the established players were Halya Ayurvedics, which owned a whole range of herbal products which were in high demand; another player was Lemne, which though small in size, had to its credit the market's best selling herbal brand, i.e., Himalaya anti-pimple cream. This cream was a success story in itself and was a highly respected brand. Apart from these, there were certain regional players.

The company decided to conduct market research, before actually entering the market. For this, a market research company was hired. According to the report presented by the agency, herbal business was a new trend in the market. More and more people wanted to shift to herbal products, instead of regular cosmetics that were largely chemical. Though the competition in this line was stiff, Halya was the market leader with 55 per cent of market share and Lemne had around 25 per cent of market share. The rest of the market was divided between other regional players. The agency also reported that the type of products manufactured by these companies was more or less similar, however they all boasted one or the other speciality, which they claimed to be their own. Being a highly nascent market, the agency predicted that there was a large segment of market share that needed to be tapped. According to the agency estimates, the company needed to make large initial investments; the research cost to develop a good product was obvious. Besides, investments had to be made not only in the plant, machinery and equipment, but also in the recruitment of new employees. Since this was a specialised field, the company needed to take a decision which was profitable not only in the short term, but was also viable in the long run.

After much deliberation, the company decided to take up the challenge. It decided to initially launch an Ayurveda cream for acne and pimples and only later extend its line of products after studying the response of the consumers. The product was named after the company Zala Ayurvedics, so as to cash upon the existing brand equity of the company. The division being an extension of the company's pharmaceutical business, the entire organisation was enthusiastic about the new product.

The investments required for the new business could have been made by borrowing from the market. However, the company decided to draw funds from its core business only. This was a major decision, as huge investments were required to be made in Ayurvedics.

To give adequate attention to the product, a new team of employees was recruited to take care of the whole division. This team was divided into three levels—the top management comprised the existing management, for the middle level and the lowest level, i.e., foremen and workers, specialised labour was recruited. A separate office and factory were also set up for Zala Ayurvedics. The recruitment procedure and the construction of the factory took almost a year. The company took another 6 months to launch Zala Ayurvedics. Large-scale preparations were made to launch it, the idea was to launch it with a bang. Major plans were drawn up to make this event a huge success.

issues ahead—promotion policy

Since Ayurvedics was a new business for the company, it had to develop a whole new distribution network for its product. Agents and distributors of the main competitors in the field were tapped and taken on their side. The company decided to launch the product initially in the metros only, to study the response of the urban market, the main target consumers. The first lot of supply of goods to distributors was kept under check and its size was intentionally kept small, though the factory had the capacity for large-scale production, if the product did well in the market.

For the initial launch and to win the loyalty of its distributors and retailers, the sales and marketing department, decided to offer 10 wristwatches to dealers who gave an order of 75 or more packs at one time as a token of appreciation and as a first step towards building a long prospective relationship. Large budgets were allocated for advertising and other sales promotion activities.

As the product was launched, it made a deep impact on the market. Since the distribution network was strong and large, it became an instant hit among the distributors. All the dealers who were approached responded positively and soon the first lot was cleared from the company's inventory. In fact, due to heavy demand, the company decided to double its production. The consumers seemed to like the product as it was promoted intensively through advertisements broadcasted on all TV channels. (However, the company was not aware of the stock position, i.e., how much was cleared from the dealer's inventory.)

the downfall

Everything was proceeding smoothly till the company representatives approached the dealers for fresh orders. They found that huge stocks had piled up with the dealers. This came as a rude shock to the company as it had produced in excess of its holding capacity. The dealers were not ready to place any new orders, whereas the company was in dire need of funds to pay back its pharmaceutical division. This marked the beginning of the downfall, which was destined. The big question facing the company was where it had gone wrong. The company had played its part well. All surveys had revealed that consumers had greatly appreciated the product as was evident from the large orders received from dealers. But the question was what was the reason for the stockpiling. Efforts were made to tackle the problem, but the piled up stock as well as the huge investment made out of the company's core business, i.e., pharmaceuticals, exacerbated the situation. To complicate matters, the news soon spread in the market that Zala Pvt. Ltd was facing a cash crunch. The brand equity and credibility of the company which had taken years to build up, was now under pressure. It was not that the entire business was dependent on Zala Ayurvedics. As mentioned earlier, this new division was launched with funds from the pharmaceutical business. 'No returns' here meant that the pharmaceutical division began to face problems in meeting its dues. This was detrimental to the company's image.

There was low morale in the organisation. The competitors began to take advantage of the situation and a new rumour about the company was heard every day, some of them being baseless. However, the company had no means to prove its innocence.

As the saying goes, when a ship drowns rats are the first to desert it; there were large scale resignations from the organisation. The resignation of the sales and marketing manager dealt the final blow to Zala Ayurvedics which was viewed as a doomed ship. Years of hard work had gone waste. The company decided to let matters lie for a while, so that the storm would subside, and people would forget the entire episode. Any new move by the company at that time would have further weakened its position.

mere survival

For nearly three months, the company ran its Ayurvedics business on a cost to cost basis without making any profits so as to clear off the stock that had piled up with the distributors and retailers. However, its own stock had to be dealt with.

Though everything appeared to be calm on the surface, investigations were underway behind the scenes. The company's insiders found that the entire operation was the brainwave of a few agents of the company along with some distributors. The mastermind behind the plan was a competitor firm which had been trying to takeover Zala's business for a very long time, but had not succeeded in its nefarious plans. The distributors and dealers were lured by watches and other personal benefits offered by the rival company. Thus, the gifts (wrist watches) which the company had planned to give to attract distributors had become the very reason for its downfall.

Many new facts surfaced over time as the investigations progressed. One such fact was that by taking advantage of the margins given to them, the distributors and agents had started price cutting. Therefore any new stock which the company supplied to the market at the original price was not accepted, as the product was available at lower prices with the dealers. The cost of each cream to the company was Rs 25, which it supplied to its agents at Rs 40. The product was delivered to the retailers at a price of Rs 60 who in turn sold it to the end-users for Rs 75.

Since the dealers had piled up huge stocks, their immediate concern was to get rid of them, as the company's new lot was ready. Thus, they were willing to sell the stock to consumers at a price of Rs 60 only. As long as they were able to cover their costs, they did not mind losing their margins, as they made profits from the watches they had received earlier. Thus, the watches were like their bonus. Moreover, with the connivance of the agents who had given an added benefit of Rs 15, they were able to make profit even after selling the goods at the same prices. This was highly detrimental to the company's image. Even the product, which had enjoyed a decent image, was adversely affected by price cutting as questions about its quality were raised. The company could not produce more as its earlier stocks had not been cleared. Further, due to stoppage in the production cycle, the labour remained idle. Even the cost of maintaining machinery that was largely imported was becoming difficult to recover. The costs were building up and so were the liabilities of the company. Things continued like this for a while, until the company decided to tackle the issue. The sales and marketing manager had already quit. The company needed someone who could not only take charge, but also tactfully handle the situation. The management considered Avinash Singh, a manager in the pharmacy department who was known for his expertise and tact in handling difficult situations.

When Avinash took charge he decided on an aggressive yet systematic plan of action. He was clear that unlike last time the department would not leave any loopholes or commit any mistakes. He decided to re-launch the cream because it had become a matter of prestige for the company. The lost reputation had to be regained. Moreover, since the culprits had been identified, Avinash decided to take action against them. Though legally they could not be caught, he decided to trap them in their own net. Major preparations were made and a few changes were made in the product to give it a completely new look.

the new plan

Avinash took special precautions in the sales and distribution plan, which had been another failure earlier. Detailed research was undertaken in this field to identify those who were likely to ditch and be disloyal to the company. Avinash kept a strict watch on all matters and recorded all the deals in detail and evaluated them later. He ensured that all orders placed by the agents were cross-checked with the orders of the sales representatives of the company before the supplies were sent. He drew up special contracts to not only identify the culprits, but also to trap them so that they could not play their dirty game again. It was made clear that only orders of certain fixed sizes (and less of course) would be entertained. Moreover, it was decided that reorders would be accepted only when the company was sure that the earlier supply had been cleared. Avinash's investigations had confirmed the fact that this whole episode had been masterminded by the rival company. To ensure that the past events were not repeated, Avinash was determined not to take any chances.

Since the whole plan was very rigid and strict, the research department suggested taking dealers into confidence and offering them some incentive to stock the product. The product had earned a bad name that needed to be cleared. The company needed to offer some extra incentive to its dealers but cost constraints prevented it from offering incentives like wristwatches as it had done in the past. By offering the watches, the company had raised the hopes of the distributors who would not have agreed to the new contract without some personal benefit. The question was how to lure them. To complicate matters, the rival companies had introduced some gift scheme for the customers. As the company's credibility was fairly low in the market it could not raise funds from there. The funds withdrawn from the pharmaceutical business had not been recovered, which adversely affected the company.

Avinash decided that the company needed to introduce the product in larger size, that is apart from the regular size tubes. It manufactured tubes of double the normal size for dealers who achieved the highest sales targets. This not only gave an incentive to the dealers, but also enabled greater coverage of the product. The second reason for this decision was that when the dealers would themselves use the product only then they would be able to compare its results with the rival company's product. Another problem that was solved in the process was that the huge stocks which lay in the godown were cleared.

victory flight

Initially, the product took time to take off, its quality gave it the necessary support, which was very much needed. Soon the product made its presence felt in the market. The company even introduced some new products. Today, its share in the herbal market is no less than that of any other company: Zala Ayurvedics controls about 35 per cent share in the herbal market. The company's lost reputation has been re-established. The credit, undoubtedly, went to Avinash Singh who tactfully handled such a stressful and difficult situation and, in the process, saved the company from inevitable doom.

Tanya's Dilemma*

Tanya was one of the lucky few in her college affiliated to Lucknow University to have been selected by a prestigious company during campus recruitment. She had been a consistently high performing student, excelling in group activities and leadership roles. Tanya had casually sent her resume to Anizure, but the pre-placement discussion convinced her that this was an ideal opportunity to develop her career. She did not want to study further and having a good career in Lucknow was difficult. The work seemed challenging and the move to Delhi was sure to offer good opportunities for growth. After much family discussion and her final year college exams in April 2002, Tanya joined Anizure as a customer relationship executive.

job profile

Anizure, one of the largest BPO service providers in the country, had its headquarters in Delhi and over 4,000 associates worked across five metros. It had been in operation since 2 years and its client list included top-line MNCs from across the globe, including India.

The job profile matched Tanya's interests and skills. There were some teething troubles however, considering the new work environment and the cultural shift from Lucknow to Delhi, but she managed well. A sympathetic supervisor made her transition easier. In June 2003 she was promoted to team leader, collections, and assumed the responsibility of a team of 25 customer relations executives. Around this time there was a complete overhauling of the senior management which led to the beginning of her problems.

*Acknowledgements: Anuja Chachra, Madhurim Gupta, Sunandini Pande and Tahira Nath.

organisational functioning

Anizure undertook back-end processing operations in three sectors: customer service, sales and collections (Appendix 3.1). While its client list was diversified, the bulk of the business came from a few companies. With the emergence of new BPOs, competition was stiff.

The Delhi office was headed by a senior management team, along with a group of team leaders (TL) and systems delivery leaders (SDL) who coordinated over 800 agents or customer relations executives (Appendix 3.2). Most of the employees were under 30 years of age and the work environment was vibrant and active. The emphasis was on quality work, with many incentives, including promotions, and bonuses given to star performers.

new business

In March 2003 there was a restructuring in the top management. It had been felt that while the company had had a successful start, the emphasis should shift to expansion and growth. Generating new business, increasing employee productivity and meeting higher quality standards were the new driving factors. The new management set high targets and expected a similar drive from employees.

Since her promotion in June, Tanya's responsibilities had enlarged and included a lot of operational work along with coordination of her team (Appendix 3.3). She balanced both aspects of her work, but personally preferred to spend more time with the agents because she felt that the high pressure and repetitive nature of the job could make the work monotonous. She remembered how much time she had taken to adjust when she had first joined the organisation and was grateful to her then immediate supervisor, Mr Rao, who had spent much time advising her and supporting her in the initial adjustment process.

prospective team leader

She often felt that she was unable to give the same quality time to her own agents. One such agent was Rohit, who had been recruited just 6 months ago. Although an excellent performer, he had some adjustment problems, as he had moved from Nagpur. Tanya thought Rohit had tremendous potential, and seeing his team participation strengths, had even been considering him as a prospective team leader. But Rohit often acted irresponsibly and had been reported twice to the management on charges of poor call quality. Tanya believed that this was due to high stress and expectations and wanted to discuss the issue with Rohit.

Apart from this, working in the collections department brought its own set of challenges. Traditionally considered the most difficult department to work in, it involved agents making calls as reminders, and negotiating with the clients regarding late payments and defaults. Since many clients did not or could not pay, making a successful call was often difficult. Agents found it tough to handle the stress, especially when clients became angry or abusive. Employee burnout and attrition were the highest in this department in the company as compared with sales and customer relations that were relatively low pressure areas. Added to this was the pressure of working night shifts and long durations at a stretch. Agents often complained about health problems and difficulty in maintaining a balanced family and social life. Tanya thought that the current training period for agents was not adequate. Mr Rao was the manager of the training department and she often discussed with him of how cultural sensitivity and discussion and participation groups would equip agents to handle their job better.

daily challenges

While Tanya enjoyed her work and the daily challenges it brought, she was often stressed out and unable to cope with the continuous pressure. The problems were largely related to dealing with the expectations and targets set by her immediate supervisor, Mr Malhotra, who had been appointed recently.

Mr Malhotra had joined Anizure after working for 8 years in the sales department of a major FMCG company. He was appointed to ensure that the high quality standards that were required could be achieved and sustained. The high sales growth figures he had achieved in his last job were instrumental in bringing him to Anizure. He believed that the strategies he had used in his previous organisation would work here as well. He equated a higher number of call services with higher sales and believed that pressure and tight deadlines were the best methods to ensure high employee productivity. He insisted on adopting a direct leadership role and often by passed the team leaders to interact directly with the agents and take continuous reports.

basic strategy

Although the call volume had increased marginally since Mr Malhotra assumed charge, Tanya thought that the basic strategy used was flawed and was worried about the future of her team members. She was aware that attrition rates had always been high in this industry, and agents would not hesitate to look for alternatives at the slightest provocation. She had brought up this issue with Mr Malhotra and discussed options to implement more employee-oriented measures to raise employee morale. He rejected most of her suggestions and added that as long as call volumes were increasing there was no reason for low employee morale (Appendix 3.4). Tanya retaliated and openly criticized the current management policies.

In August 2003 Anizure undertook an employee audit, and for the first time, all employees were asked to give feedback about the working environment and individual job satisfaction. The results of the survey revealed that employee satisfaction was low, and most of the employees did not feel motivated to work or innovate. It was also found that work pressure was too high and many employees rated their relationship with their team leaders as unsatisfactory or poor.

work environment

Tanya believed that this was a direct fall-out of the lack of time spent with each agent by the team leaders as well as the inflexible work environment. She planned to discuss this matter with Mr Malhotra at the earliest. However, before she had an opportunity to do so there was an employee service complaint. Rohit was involved in a quality issue vis-à-vis an important client. Mr Malhotra was determined to fire Rohit as this was the third complaint against him. Tanya, on the other hand, believed that this would mean losing a capable agent, who could be corrected by just a reprimand.

Tanya was in a dilemma. She believed that Mr Malhotra was wrong to be so harsh with Rohit. On the other hand, she was also concerned about the high standards of quality the company had achieved and could not jeopardize the company's reputation. She had to submit Rohit's work appraisal, which would decide his future.

APPENDIX 3.1: WORKING AT A CALL CENTRE

Anizure handles back-end processing operations for clients like insurance companies, credit card operations and industrial businesses. Three basic services are provided—customer relations, which involves collecting feedback, answering enquiries and providing information about the client's business operations; sales, which includes making sales enquiries and pitches to prospective customers who may be interested in a specific product or service; collections, which involves contacting customers who have not paid or defaulted on their bills and need to be reminded about their due payment.

Agents work in 8-hour shifts and are given pre-assigned breaks and have a strictly monitored call schedule. Since most call centres in India work with US-based clients, call centre operations start in the evening and continue throughout the night. Each agent attends 60–100 calls daily, with the frequency depending on the day of the week and the time of the year. Every call is recorded and a sample is analysed to ensure that it is conforming to required standards.

Calls are assessed on two criteria:

Duration of the Call

The time taken by each agent on a call is called the average handling time (AHT). Since the purpose is to maximise call volumes, there is constant pressure on the agents to reduce the AHT. The AHT for customer service calls is 200 seconds, while the AHT for collection calls is 360 seconds as there is more negotiation required.

Quality of the Call

Apart from the post-call quality control done at the centre, at the end of each call, the customer is asked if he/she wants to give feedback, and the feedback is taken by an automatic voice response system. Calls are analysed on the basis of overall satisfaction, agent knowledge, ease of understanding and account knowledge.

Each call is rated for the level of satisfaction. A score of 75 per cent and above satisfaction level is considered adequate though a score above this minimum level is more appreciated. Clients can also lodge quality complaints against any particular agent if the agent fails to meet optimum quality standards.

APPENDIX 3.2: ORGANISATIONAL STRUCTURE

The Vice President, operations, is part of the management team that heads the company. There are seven systems delivery leaders

(SDL) spread across the three divisions; three SDLs handle customer relations, two are in charge of collections and two of sales. SDLs are supported by the training division, which is responsible for the agents' training. There are 35 team leaders. Each SDL has seven team leaders reporting to him/her. The team leader is in charge of 15–25 call agents.

Appendix 3.3: Tanya's Job Profile

A team leader's goals and responsibilities include:

- Leading a team of 15–20 customer relations executives or agents.
- Goal setting, performance reviews and development plan for all direct reports.
- Responsibility for day-to-day functioning/administrative work, including production floor management.
- Responsibility for delivery of all customer quality matrices as per goals.

Appendix 3.4: Collections Call Volumes: January–August 2003

Month 2003	Number of Calls	% Satisfactory
January	56,250	88.54
February	53,460	86.32
March	64,285	81.08
April	64,310	80.90
May	64,300	81.02
June	63,780	79.60
July	64,530	79.32
August	63,580	80.01

BLAZE MOTOR CORPORATION*

The alarm clock went off at 6 a.m. in A-6, Panchvati Apartments, Ambawadi, Ahmedabad. Ajay Srivastav had set the alarm early and quickly got up at this unusual hour. As he hurried through his normal routine, his mind repeatedly ran through his day's plan. He had planned to spend his weekend in a manner unusual for a regional sales manager of a leading passenger car company in the country. After much deliberation, he was going against the directives given by his superior for the first time. He was planning to personally interview some people who had switched from a Blaze Motor Corporation car to another company's car.

background—Ajay Srivastav

Ajay was a brilliant student and had completed his MBA (marketing) in 2000 from one of the top management schools in the country in Bangalore. He had got a job with LLH, one of the leading, FMCG companies in India. Working to his full potential, he soon became the area sales manager, Delhi. After a while he realised that the scope for further promotion and growth within the organisation was limited. He began to examine other alternatives and applied for marketing jobs in various top organisations. He received a number of offers but finally decided to join Blaze Motor Corporation (BMC) which had been the market leader in the passenger car segment for the last two decades. He joined BMC as regional sales manager, Ahmedabad, in August 2002.

emergence as a market leader

The year 1981 saw the dawn of a new era in the Indian passenger car market with the incorporation of Blaze Motor Corporation.

*Acknowledgements: Dheeraj Renganath, Joypratip Sengupta, Namita Shah, Rohit Saraogi and Savita Subramaniyam.

The company revolutionised the market with the introduction of international technology and style matched by superior performance through its collaboration with a leading Japanese automobile company. Soon BMC became synonymous with the small and medium car segments in India. BMC was able to garner more than three-fourths of the passenger car market share in a short span. It also created many new segments within the market with the introduction of newer models that became extremely popular.

But towards the late 1990s, with the entry of several major foreign players in the market, BMC's market share declined marginally though sales continued to increase. BMC did not perceive this as a major concern since it was still the market leader and market surveys conducted previously had indicated that the consumer thought highly of the company. It was at this point that Ajay joined the Ahmedabad office of BMC.

surface calm

Initially, he was overwhelmed by the magnitude of his responsibilities of handling the marketing strategy of the company in western India. To add to this, the team of middle level managers reporting to him, going by the prevalent work culture at BMC, shied away from taking any initiative and expected to be given comprehensive instructions regarding policy and strategy. This hierarchical and relatively inflexible style of operation was reflective of BMC's functioning during the last two decades. The practice was also evident in the quarterly senior management meetings held at the BMC headquarters in Gurgaon.

After a month of joining BMC, Ajay had the opportunity to interact with the other four RSMs and the GM at the second quarterly meeting at Gurgaon. He received a warm welcome and was initiated and introduced to the procedures followed at such meetings by the GM, Mr Jagdish Lal. Being a new entrant, he was not expected to present a first quarterly report but to view this as an experience. Ajay's role was reduced to that of an observer and he was quite impressed with the quarterly figures of the other four regions. Mr Lal was satisfied with the sales figures and indicated to all the RSMs to continue implementing their aggressive marketing strategy.

After the meeting Mr Lal had a private meeting with Ajay, he asked him about his experience so far and then elaborated on his vision for BMC in the coming years. He expected Ajay and the other RSMs to adopt a common strategy for consolidation of the market share of BMC's flagship brands like Blaze-800 and Blaze ZDx. Ajay left Gurgaon with a clear-cut objective and specific targets to meet.

the ripples appear

In line with the GM's guidelines, Ajay introduced a promotional campaign for Blaze ZDx. He called it the 'Diwali Blaze Bonanza' wherein anyone purchasing a Blaze ZDx from October would get a discount of 10 per cent. Expecting a positive response to the scheme, Ajay began to conceptualise similar promotional campaigns for other Blaze cars. However, on 7 November 2002 when his area sales manager presented him with the monthly sales report, Ajay was shocked. Not only did the sales of Blaze ZDx not show a significant increase, but also whatever increase was seen was less than that during the corresponding period in the previous year.

Ajay spent a sleepless night wondering why his strategy had failed and decided to call an emergency meeting of his sales team the next day. Feeling personally responsible, he visited the primary dealer in Ahmedabad who had not withdrawn his scheme and observed the prospective customers. He approached an apparently irate person leaving the outlet and introduced himself as a prospective Blaze buyer. He tried to elicit the customer's views on the purchase of the Blaze ZDx under the scheme. He was taken aback by the response:

> I came to enquire about the Blaze Bolano and not to purchase the Blaze ZDx. Why would I purchase a car which is a spruced-up

version of what my father bought years ago? As regards the discount, the company has probably compromised on the quality any way. Blaze 800, it's not even qualified to be called a car and I wouldn't buy either even if the discount offered was 20 per cent.

A stunned Ajay immediately withdrew the scheme fearing that it had a negative impact on the consumer.

After two weeks of analysing the figures and talking to a few more customers, Ajay realised that the problem was more serious than the marginal decline in market share. Prospective customers no longer considered a Blaze car to be a status symbol or thought it offered value for money. It appeared to him that BMC had not built up on its first-mover advantage by going in for product innovation; rather it had rested on its laurels and hoped for the best.

Since the next quarterly meeting was a month away, Ajay requested an immediate video conferencing with Mr Lal who was in Japan to discuss a collaboration deal with a Japanese engine manufacturer. The latter was already aware of the promotional scheme. Ajay briefed him about the steps he had undertaken for the failed scheme. At this point, Mr Lal questioned him about his assumption of the failure of the scheme and told him not to jump to premature conclusions. He disagreed with Ajay on this and told him that the scheme should have been implemented for more time. He also reprimanded Ajay for having spoken personally to customers at an outlet as he believed that this could have degraded the company's image. Mr Lal ended the conversation by asking Ajay to refrain from taking such measures and assured him that there was no serious issue to be dealt with. Ajay was not at all convinced by Mr Lal's arguments and felt that action was imperative. Keeping in mind that a third quarterly meeting was scheduled for next month, Ajay decided to present his case for a policy change at that forum. This time he would be prepared with supporting data. For this purpose, he decided to prepare two reports of customers who had shifted from a Blaze car. The profiles and data collected from the customers he interviewed are provided in Appendix 3.5.

APPENDIX 3.5

consumer case 1: Varun and Anu—the new generation

Varun is doing his postgraduation in communications from a reputed institute. He has an interest in cars and machines and is popular for the storehouse of information that he has on the subject. Whenever a relative or friend wanted to buy a car, Varun was contacted.

Anu, Varun's close friend, was contemplating to buy a car. She lived with her parents and younger sister. She wanted a car that was economical and convenient for a small family. She called Varun and asked his advice on the various models available in the market. They soon met to discuss her requirements in detail. Anu's objective was that the whole family should be able to drive the car with ease. As she was tall she wanted ample leg space. Value for money and low maintenance cost were high on her priority list. Varun recommended the Blaze ZDx. His suggestion was based on his 5 years experience with the ZDx. The model gave good mileage and was arguably the best city car. He was more than satisfied with the servicing and the service coverage. The flip side was its limited luggage space, which Anu did not consider as very important. However, Varun did not prefer driving long distance at high speeds in the ZDx because the steering shook at high speed levels. On the whole, he was very happy with the car and faced no major problems with it. By then Anu was clear about purchasing a ZDx.

Anu noticed a Hyundai Accent outside Varun's house and inquired about it. Varun had purchased the Accent because he wanted a luxury car. Anu jokingly questioned his loyalty towards Blaze cars and he shot back saying that purchase depended a lot on individual perceptions. He perceived Blaze as a company that offers cars for the middle class. Though Blaze Bolano belonged to the luxury segment, he found its design pathetic. Since the model itself did not impress him, he did not bother to find out about the machinery. The advertisements asserting that the air conditioning was better than that of other cars did not appeal to him either. Moreover, Bolano parts were expensive and were available only at limited service centres. He believed that a luxury car should be high on comfort, have a powerful steering, plush interiors, full-fledged accessories and an awesome design that makes onlookers say 'Wow!'. He expected a car to be equipped with an emergency and a tool kit. Bolano did not meet these standards. Based on these criteria he had short-listed two cars—the Accent and the Honda City. The Honda City's spare parts were very expensive. Moreover, Varun was impressed by the hospitality and the effectiveness of the Hyundai salespeople. He also found the Accent's features far better than those of other models available in the market.

Anu asked him what his decision would have been had Blaze launched some promotions or offered spare parts at lower prices. Varun said that promotions, especially price discounts, did not matter to him, particularly in the high value car segment. But additional distinctive features did. Anu got a lot of insight into the various aspects of purchasing a car. Varun offered to drop her back home and gave her a choice between the ZDx and the Accent. Anu chuckled and replied, 'Let me feel my would-be possession.'

consumer case 2: Dr Raj's shift in loyalty

Dr Deepak Raj was sitting at his study making a note of a few tasks that he had to do. Slightly tense, he looked at the big wall clock as it struck 10 a.m. He was supposed to deliver a lecture on Organisational Behaviour at 2 p.m. at the most reputed management school in Ahmedabad. Though he was well prepared and confident for the lecture, another problem was disturbing him. The new Blaze ZDx car he had bought a year back was giving him trouble. And as luck would have it, the car did not start that morning when he went to drop his wife at her office. This was his last lecture and it was very important for him to take the class.

Also, there was no alternative mode of transport available as the institute which was located in the suburbs.

He called up the Service Centre, the largest service station for BMC in Ahmedabad, and asked for a mechanic to be sent immediately. He then recollected his friend Vinod Shah's experience at the same centre where he had sent his ZDx for servicing. When he collected his car, he sensed some problem. He had the car serviced again at another service station and found that a few of its parts had been changed or removed without his knowledge. Recalling this incident, Dr Raj was reluctant to get the car serviced in his absence. When the mechanic arrived, Dr Raj made sure that he checked the car in his presence. After half an hour the mechanic told him that there were some major engine problems which could only be rectified at the service station. They both drove to the service centre which was near by. One hour later the car was repaired.

proper value

Dr Raj had an emotional attachment to his earlier Blaze 800 because it was his first car. He bought the ZDx not because of any concrete reason but only because he wanted a change. However, being the owner of Blaze ZDx did not make him feel proud. The car did not give him similar value as his Blaze 800. He described the car as a 'scooter of larger size'. If ever he thought of going on a vacation with his family, he was not confident taking the Blaze ZDx. It had limited luggage room and, more importantly, while travelling long distances the car lost its smooth pace. Often the company's service people had difficulty in identifying the problems.

Hence Dr Raj thought of purchasing a car that offered better technology and additional features, preferably a foreign brand in the same segment. He thought that a foreign car would assure him of quality and service, though he was sceptical about the service network and the availability of spare parts. At the dinner table, Dr Raj shared this idea with his family. His wife suggested that since they already owned a small car they should buy a luxury car. His children were excited about this suggestion and began to list all the possible cars. They shortlisted three: Ford Ikon, Opel Astra and Mahindra Scorpio.

FUTURE OF A BRILLIANT MANAGER*

Anand was sitting at the window seat of the plane, Mumbai gliding past below him. There was no sign of happiness on his face. His financial services firm was not doing well and was on the verge of pulling out its major service offering from the market.

Anand's background

Anand was a management graduate from the Premier Institute, Pune, with specialisation in marketing. He belonged to Mumbai where he lived in a joint family. He had recently got married and his wife was a housewife.

During campus recruitment he had joined a marketing company with a stint in Bangalore. After 2 years he decided to move back to Mumbai and explore openings in upcoming fields and upgrade his existing skills. His efforts paid off and he got an opportunity to work in a financial research firm, Financial Research and Marketing Company (FRMC). The job not only offered good perks, but also a chance to develop international contacts. Anand was extremely happy, working in Mumbai and staying with his family.

*Acknowledgements: Atul Rohan Garg, Deepak Singh, Garima Gupta, Rashmi Wadhwa, Traptika Chauhan.

FRMC

FRMC, a US-based company, had established its credentials in the Indian financial research market. Market liberalisation and a booming financial market were compelling factors that had made the company look to India as a good market. The headquarters in Indian were in Mumbai. The company dealt in various financial instruments like options, mutual fund, stock market analysis and debt instruments. Most products were developed in-house. It catered to various segments of the financial market with several standard applications and software for small institutional customers and customised solutions for the large institutional customers in the financial market. FRMC was sales driven and had fully developed sales, product development, research and development, and IT departments.

new service

After establishing itself in the country FRMC had come up with an innovative service concept. The idea was to provide share price in real time through a pager service. The targeted customers were frequent travellers with an interest in the financial market. The launching of the service was approved after extensive research and prolonged deliberations across departments. Initially the service was to be restricted to Mumbai, with only the quotes of stock market prices being made available in real time. The geographical coverage and nature of services was expected to be expanded after testing its viability in the market. A special pager was to be provided for those availing of the service. The concept had been a huge success in the international market. As it was yet to be introduced in India by any company, FRMC had the first mover advantage.

The service had been conceptualised about a year before Anand was appointed product manager. The previous product manager had begun work on the concept, but several problems had arisen.

Though successful and very cost effective in other countries, particularly in the UK and Singapore, the same business model did not appear viable in India.

Anand and the environment

The induction programme for a new employee at FRMC is for a minimum of two weeks, but Anand's training was completed in a week. He had two subordinates directly reporting to him and helping him provide service support. There were many problems and time and resources were limited. Anand had to deal with the internal environment comprising his team, the organisational system and the burden of a non-performing service. Outside the organisation, the government regulations and vendors involved in the service had to be managed. Being one of the youngest and least experienced members of the organisation, he had the burden of proving his worth and justifying the faith the company had reposed in him.

pre-launch scenario

As soon as he joined, Anand was given a deadline of 6 months to work out a viable strategy for launching the product in the market. As the work was not in his domain of expertise, he had to put in extra effort to do the work well. He not only had to launch the service successfully, but also had to strategise its long-term performance.

requisite frequency

Providing the service to the end-customer on a pager required a particular broadband frequency that was not available in India. FRMC had to obtain government permission and set up the required infrastructure to provide the frequency for commercial purposes. Anand and his team studied the rules and regulations and initiated the paper work to have things in place. The cost of this was high. Getting permission turned out to be a long-drawn process. They hired a consultant with extensive experience in the telecom industry to find an alternative approach. After 5 months of experimentation and research, he suggested a process to launch the service through the frequency currently available in the Indian market.

This solution had its advantages and disadvantages. The advantage was the enormous financial saving of the budget allotted for setting up the infrastructure. The drawback was that the large number of pagers that had been ordered by the previous product manager could not be used at the available frequency.

hardware requirements

One problem was solved. But with only 3 months to go before the launch of the service, more problems cropped up. Ordering new handsets to receive the existing frequency was both costly and time consuming. Anand and his team proposed an innovative solution. After studying the components and chip design of a pager with the help of the R&D department, they suggested the insertion of an additional chip in the pagers already lying in the warehouse. With the insertion of this chip the handsets would receive the desired frequency. This was a better and economical solution than ordering a new lot of pager handsets.

another crisis

The rigorous pace of work affected the team's personal and social lives. The project suffered a setback when one of the team members quit the job. Anand had no choice but continue with the work with one assistant, while the company recruited another person who could competently handle the work at that late stage.

problems continue

A few hundred pagers were required to test market the service. The manufacturer needed a lead time of 3 months to add the new chip and deliver the instruments in India. No pager manufacturer based in India could help them. Anand and a team member went to Australia to meet the manufacturer and negotiate the production time. He reduced it by 1 month, but the CEO of FRMC had to be convinced to extend the launch date.

plan of action

With just a month to go before the launch, the instruments had to be delivered, test marketing had to be done, field staff had to be trained, target markets had to be identified and a concrete marketing plan had to be in place. Desperate, Anand decided to give it a shot and ask for more time. Much to his relief, the CEO agreed to extend the date by a month.

service launch

Anand began work on the product launch. The money saved from other heads was diverted to bring in international trainers for the FRMC sales team and for an increased advertising budget. The service was test marketed for a month before being released. For the first time FRMC was launching a service targeted at the non-institutional customer. It was to be a new and challenging experience for FRMC.

The introductory offer was a subscription charge of Rs 2,000, which included a handset and stock market information for a month. From the second month onwards the customer could get information for a monthly payment of Rs 250. FRMC expected to make a decent profit if the sales forecasts were met. The salespersons received a commission of Rs 250 for every subscription sold.

post-launch scenario

Around the time of the launch a new CEO from FRMC's US office replaced the present one. The new CEO had earlier worked with the head of the sales department for 2 years in their US operations and both shared a good rapport. Meanwhile, Anand was happy with the way the project had turned out. He saw a bright future for himself in the company.

Unfortunately, the product did not do well in the market. Except for initial curiosity, the customers did not show much interest. The expected demand and popularity never happened. Despite Anand and his team's 3 months of hard work, they could not gain any market. Considering the state of affairs, the new CEO called the team and asked it to submit an assessment report. The specific areas to be covered were:

- What went wrong in the process, starting from conceptualising the service to launching it in the market; the specific problem points.
- The plan of action regarding the sustainability of the service.

The report was to determine if the service should continue in the market or be withdrawn immediately.

DIFFICULT TRANSITIONS*

Rajul had been working for New Solution Technology (NST) Company for the last 5 years. NST, a software development company, provided software consulting services to corporations. Its clientele included mainly US-based multinational firms like Texas

*Acknowledgements: Anshul Sushil, Ayan Bhattacharya, Gaurava Singh and Sandeep Mishra.

Instruments, IBM Corporation and US Postal Services. The company was just 2 years old but had gained prominence through ingenious and innovative products such as NSTCube, Flexi97, Super2Xs, Gen-Tech and ContolExpo.

growth and learning

Rajul's experience with the company was good from day one. The job met his expectations and he grew with the organisation. His work was recognised and appreciated. The company was decentralised and the staff enjoyed much autonomy and freedom. The communication channels were transparent and the workplace had an open culture. During meetings everyone was free to express their ideas without any pressure of hierarchy. Rajul recalled the first meeting he had attended when he was just a week old in the company. It was an important meeting to discuss the interface base for the SolvSoft ERP package the company was developing. Initially, Rajul was hesitant to put forward his ideas, but Mr Sukumar, his project leader, put him at ease. He was introduced as, 'Ladies and gentlemen, please welcome Rajul, the fresh brain who is here to give some freshness to our old and stale thoughts.'

Mr Sukumar, 40, was experienced and well known in the field. Through his hard work and innovative approach, Rajul got along very well with Mr Sukumar. He was sad when the latter was sent to the offshore headquarters of the MNC for the project's implementation. Nevertheless, he was happy to have had the chance to learn under such a remarkable person; for him, Mr Sukumar was a respected mentor.

The other team members were also nice and got along very well. Rajul and three other colleagues often went out together for lunch on weekends. The new project leader, Mr Kulkarni, was very down-to-earth, helping them whenever they needed it without being obtrusive.

good times end

Like all good things, this phase too came to an end. Recession in the software sector, coupled with 9/11 and compounding losses, had made survival difficult. Projects on which negotiations were going on were scrapped. Ongoing projects suffered, with clients looking to cut costs. At that time Rajul's project was in its preliminary stages. Following 9/11 the client withdrew the project. To cut costs the company decided to lay off developers working on that project. When news of the shutdown broke, he was devastated; for him, nothing could replace NST. Fortunately, Rajul's experience and recommendations enabled him to find another position easily. He found a comparable position at United Technology (UT).

'Comparable' was probably the wrong word. UT and NST were as different as they could be. The top managers at UT were least concerned about individual performance. Promotions and rewards were based on length of service and how well employees got along with their seniors.

differences of opinion

The project he was assigned to was for developing a banking software. Given his earlier experience he was comfortable with it; but not for long. In the brainstorming session he got a taste of how things worked in the company. Mr Das, the project leader (PL), was around the same age as Rajul and had similar experience. During the meeting Rajul proposed the use of Linux for the development of the software. Because of cost constraints Linux was more feasible than Microsoft products. Moreover, the software was less prone to virus attacks as hackers generally targeted the popular Microsoft. But Mr Das completely overruled his idea. According to him, Microsoft had wider applicability and was more user-friendly. He did not pay heed to Rajul's logic and the meeting ended with the decision in favour of Microsoft.

After that incident Rajul noticed that Mr Das invariably tried to insult him by denigrating his ideas. Rajul once heard him commenting to a colleague, 'Some new people think that they know everything and they forget the difference between a senior and a junior.' Rajul was aware this remark referred to his behaviour during the meeting. He was reminded of Mr Sukumar and the good times he had at NST.

establishing a rapport

Rajul's other team members were Puja, Himanshu and Rakesh. Rajul had more experience than them in software development and they usually consulted him and took his advice whenever a problem arose. They shared a good rapport and even went out for movies and dinner after work.

Because of this Rajul liked his job. His problem was only in relation to the project leader. Mr Das never attended the meetings held to discuss software development. He was never around for consultation and the responsibility fell on Rajul to help others. Gradually he began to gain importance and earned the respect of his colleagues. Mr Das was the PL of two other projects. Members of the other teams also approached Rajul for advice. The PL's attitude of ridiculing and finding fault as compared with Rajul's empathetic approach made him popular with the staff. Whenever he went to Mr Das with some idea, he was invariably snubbed and even ridiculed in front of others. Rajul realised that all this was the result of his growing popularity within the organisation and Mr Das's sense of insecurity.

Every month Mr Das submitted a progress report of all the projects under him to the Chief Executive Officer, Mr Agarwal. When the next monthly report was due, he called Rajul to his office. When Rajul entered, Mr Das was on the phone with a friend. He did not even ask Rajul to sit down and kept him waiting for almost 15 minutes. When he was through, he turned to him:

Mr Das: The project does not seem to be going in the right direction, Rajul.

Rajul: But Sir, we are working day and night and doing our best.

Mr Das: Then, Rajul, your best is not enough for the project. Please get serious.

Rajul: Excuse me, Sir! All the members are working day and night.

Mr Das: Do not get me started, Rajul. I have received information that you and your group are always out for parties and dinners instead of working on the project.

Rajul: But I do not believe that I have done something wrong and I do not think I should be giving reasons for my working style.

Mr Das: Rajul, I want everything done according to my rules.

Rajul: Sir, I think we all are working by the rules of this organisation, and we do not need to change our mode of working.

Mr Das: I think you have intentions of leaving this place very soon. Right, Rajul?

Rajul: Sir, I do not care! What I do care about is that my work should have my best and I will continue doing it.

After that interaction Rajul became more cautious of Mr Das. He knew that each action of his was being observed. Outwardly, Mr Das completely ignored Rajul. Everybody knew there was something wrong between them. Mr Das was also the acting head of the company as Mr Agarwal had gone abroad on some work. One day Rajul reached the office and found Puja crying in her cubicle. Upon being asked, she told Rajul that Mr Das had scolded her in front of everyone because she had advocated Rajul's idea.

time to leave

Things were coming to a head. Rajul could not continue working in such an atmosphere. He decided to leave for better opportunities. He received a good response to his applications. Soon he got a worthwhile offer that matched his expectations. It was time to move on.

4

corporate governance

Expected Learning Outcomes

♦ *Appreciate the role of corporate governance in affecting organ-isational dynamics to protect the interests of the stakeholders.*

♦ *Comprehend corporate trust and autonomy as main anchors of corporate governance in creating a pull and push factor in organisational dynamics.*

♦ *Distinguish between effective and ineffective corporate governance practices.*

Enron, World Com Inc. and Arthur Anderson collapsed after reaching the peak of corporate performance. In India, a number of trusted cooperative sector banks collapsed overnight. In a panic run, customers queued up outside these banks to withdraw their deposits. The reason was that the boards had betrayed the trust of their stakeholders. The illegal lending of customers' money to certain groups of individuals with suspect credentials went against the ethics of corporate governance as advocated by the system.

The fall of these powerful corporations is testimony to the importance of the corporate governance system over individual board members, the CEOs and the management. Corporate governance is defined as 'a system and a means by which a company's stakeholders direct and control its business operations' (Becker, Huselid and Ulrich, 2001). It directs every one who is directly or indirectly accountable for managing the company's affairs by way of providing strategic directions, allocating or reallocating resources, policy guidelines, and evaluating and monitoring corporate performance to protect the interests of its stakeholders and maintain their core values and ethics (Butcher and Clarke, 2002).

ROLE OF CORPORATE GOVERNANCE

Corporate governance can lead to both good and bad occurrences in an organisation. This can cause a major roadblock to building organisational capabilities to quickly respond to the changing environmental demands. The role of corporate governance is extremely critical and challenging in a geographically dispersed company operating with a multi-product profile. The policy systems of corporate governance formulated at the parent company level may not be relevant to other divisions or their operations in other countries due to variations in the social–cultural environment (Johnson and Macy, 2001). Corporate governance needs to therefore empower the company's management at each level of the organisational system for creatively responding to rapidly changing demands of the external environment. It is important that the corporate governance system facilitates in creating a strong sense of corporate values and support it through dynamic systems and procedures. The role of corporate governance is as follows.

transparency and corporate accountability

The parameters of corporate governance are used to protect the interests of its stakeholders and to ensure that the organisation does not violate the legal system and social ethical practices. However, these very parameters may generate a lack of trust among corporate members who are responsible for their own decisions toward corporate governance and can be put under scrutiny for any likely breach. A common occurrence is the result of a decision taken in the interest of stakeholders backfiring or leading to unexpected and undesirable consequences. The role of governance is not just to enforce these parameters, but also to build a sense of trust and confidence in the members of the management for all decisions taken in the best interests of the organisation (Currall and Epstein, 2003). The important role of the corporate governance system is to enforce the parameters of corporate accountability through creating and maintaining a relationship of trust among all its stakeholders (Matson, Patiath and Shavers, 2003). In order to continue to win the confidence and trust of corporate governance, the management must ensure a continuous flow of information about the company's goals and activities and maintain transparency with the stakeholders in key decisions. Thus, the flow of information is a critical aspect of efficient and effective corporate governance.

continuous renewal and empowerment

One of the key roles of corporate governance is to ensure that the management is adequately responsive and accountable towards the rapidly changing external environment such as wars, political and economic instability, technological advances and changing needs of stakeholders. Increased reliance on providing strategic directions and evaluating and monitoring corporate accountability and performance may hamper the organisation's capacity to sustain itself in changing circumstances and in different locations of business operations. The corporate governance system needs to be adaptable and incorporate new values and corporate philosophy in the light of the changing time and needs of its stakeholders in different socio-economic cultures (Tosi, Shen and Gentry, 2003). This necessitates that the parameters for assessing corporate accountability and performance are continually redefined vis-à-vis current and future challenges that the organisation may face.

good-intentioned management framework

On account of organisational operations in multicultural environments, the relevance of the corporate governance system for well-defined parameters for corporate accountability and performance is diminishing. For example, certain practices are ethical in one culture but not in another culture. The norms formulated at the parent company level may not be suitable for business operations in another culture. In order to overcome these roadblocks to responding to cultural variations, the corporate governance system may promote good intentioned management system at the operational level of the organisation. Under this framework, the management of a company is enabled to follow new strategies and values that are relevant to the needs of stakeholders in the local context. This approach equips managers to pursue plans of action which may not follow directly from the established strategic framework of the parent company. The top management needs to be reoriented and sensitised toward the possible variation in the established framework for corporate governance in the local context. It should empower local managers to use their creative potential in effectively dealing with the unpredictable nature of the business environment. The role of the corporate governance system is to help the management establish flexible organisational systems with interpersonal maturity in making more objective judgements of a given situation.

ISSUES IN ORGANISATIONAL DYNAMICS

In this age of information economy, the role of corporate governance has become more sensitive than ever as a means to enforce corporate accountability for improving its performance. As a result of the increased flow of information, corporate governance plays a key role in affecting organisational dynamics. Managers accountable for the performance of an organisation face several constraints because of the corporate governance system.

1. Corporate governance creates a two-way network of the power of pulls and pushes in an organisational system. On the one hand, it consistently forces the top management of a company to foster a higher quality of decision-making and actions by enforcing internal norms and values, rules and regulations, policies and procedures. On the other, the very intent of corporate governance limits the use of the creative potential and entrepreneurial initiative of many managers as it creates narrow, rigid and bureaucratic pathways for decisions and actions by the company's management.

2. Because of the stringent norms of corporate accountability, the top management is almost compelled to impose inflexible parameters for controlling operations by the lower management. This often leads to a lack of trust in relationships between the top and lower management. Often the process of monitoring initiates power play and politics in the organisation. Due to lack of interpersonal understanding, managers use the norms laid down by the corporate governance system as a lever to pull each other down for personal gains. Such power play and politics may cause extreme frustration and lead to attrition among employees.

3. Corporate governance expects every member to behave in accordance with the company's image, values and philosophy through its administrative procedures and adherence to local laws. This limits the autonomy of managers to take decisions in response to a new situation. They also fear that senior managers may hold them accountable for their action even when it is intended for the best interest of the company.

Such a situation hampers the initiative and problem-solving capacity of managers.

4. Managers are questioned depending upon how the top management perceives their actions and/or position that they hold in the organisation. Organisational politics also influence the perception of a manager as having taken the right or wrong action. The apprehension of being reprimanded is high especially when they are dealing with a crisis. As a result, managers constantly remain under fear for being questioned for violating the trust of corporate governance and develop a sense of insecurity and experience stress.

5. Because of these 'pulls and pushes', powerful members of the organisation victimise the weaker ones through such means as sexual harassment and undue exploitation by luring them with promotions and other benefits. The actual manipulators may escape while innocent employees may get trapped by circumstances. People experience value conflict in many situations but are largely helpless in improving the state of affairs. In such a situation, managers resort to revolt against the organisational system, quit the job, or succumb to the demands of the situation. This fosters an attitude of lack of trust in other colleagues or subordinates.

An inflexible organisational system restricts managers in the execution of strategies in sync with the local context. A strong organisational value system supported by a flexible mode of governance will empower employees to deal with the changing environmental demands.

The two cases under this module illustrate how managers struggle to maintain their integrity toward the corporate governance system against power politics in the organisation.

'A Tightrope Walk' is about an employee in the department of defence. He was assigned the additional duty of managing the staff canteen as an honorary secretary. He enthusiastically took the initiative to streamline the work of the canteen but was shocked to find a staff member openly flouting the rules. When he took action against the offender in accordance with the rules, he was accused of disrupting the functioning of the department.

'The Saga of 4P' describes the case of a manager who made personal sacrifices in the interest of the company's business and implemented innovative marketing strategies. Threatened by the success of a female manager, her superior held her responsible for tampering with the image of the company and tried to transfer her to another branch outside the country.

References

Becker, E. Brian, Huselid, Mark A. and Ulrich, Dave. (2001). *The HR scorecard: Linking people, strategy, and performance*, Boston, MA: Harvard Business School Press.

Butcher, David and Clarke, Martin. (2002). Organizational politics: The cornerstone for organizational democracy. *Organizational Dynamics, 31*(1), 35–46.

Currall, Steven C. and Epstein, Marc J. (2003). The fragility of organizational trust. *Organizational Dynamics, 32*(2), 193–206.

Johnson, Douglas B. and Macy, Granger. (2001). Using environmental paradigms to understand and change an organization's response to stakeholders. *Journal of Organizational Change Management, 14*(4), 314–334.

Matson, Eric, Patiath, Pradip and Shavers, Tim. (2003). Stimulating knowledge sharing: Strengthening your organization's internal knowledge market. *Organizational Dynamics, 32*(3), 275–285.

Tosi, Henry L., Shen, Wei and Gentry, Richard J. (2003). Why outsiders on board can't solve the corporate governance problem. *Organizational Dynamics, 32*(2), 180–192.

CASES ON CORPORATE GOVERNANCE*

key learnings

♦ *Evaluate the dynamics of power play in organisations between de facto and de jure decision makers.*

♦ *Demonstrate power struggles that managers face because of the constant intervention of the top management.*

♦ *Identify issues of discrimination that women managers face.*

♦ *Evaluate the consequences of political interference in the promotion of employees.*

A TIGHTROPE WALK

The beach was calm and only a few people were around when Lieutenant Vishal Gupta started out for a walk. He was engrossed in his thoughts, reflecting on the times since he joined the Indian Navy. Vishal joined the Indian Navy in 1994 as an air traffic control (ATC) officer. Upon completion of his training, he joined the Goa airport. His immediate boss, the senior air traffic control officer (SATCO), was Commander R.K. Sharma. Vishal was a capable controller and soon earned the respect of his colleagues.

Acknowledgements: Ajay Nayar, Amit Tripathi, Sanjukta Ghosh and Vivek Saraswat.

His commanding officer, Captain Rajeev Sinha, was very happy with his performance.

primary duty

Vishal soon realised that in the Navy one had to assume additional responsibilities not directly related to the profession. The officers' mess of the station was in a bad shape and Captain Sinha wanted something to be done about it. He called Vishal to his office and told him, 'Vishal, I want some improvement in the service and overall image of the officers' mess. Will you take charge of it as the honorary mess secretary? You have to report to Cdr S Bajaj.' 'Definitely, Sir. I'll do my best to come up to your expectations,' Vishal responded enthusiastically.

As soon as he took charge Vishal realised that the mess was in need of a turnaround. He introduced changes aimed at tackling these issues. After seeking suggestions from the officers he introduced changes in the menu, purchased new crockery and cutlery, curtains and furniture to make the mess cleaner, efficient and more appealing. Get-togethers were organised for the officers' families. He streamlined the expenses by checking the wastage of food, electricity and water. His efforts were appreciated by all the officers. Captain Sinha was particularly happy as not only was the mess functioning more efficiently, but also there were increased savings.

work conflicts

However, the responsibility of managing the mess along with his ATC duties soon became difficult for Vishal. The timings for his ATC duties were not fixed; they varied according to the flying operations at the air station. At times he had to report for duty at a short notice even in the middle of the night. Two of the officers of the department who had recently been transferred were yet to be replaced and therefore work pressure was high. Somehow he managed to perform his duties by compromising on his leisure time and his sleep.

One day Cdr Bajaj informed him that he had awarded a contract for landscaping the mess gardens to an outside agency. He asked Vishal to coordinate with the contractor for proper execution of the task and to ensure that sufficient water was available for the plants. 'This is going to be tough', thought Vishal. Water supply was scarce and he was facing difficulty in ensuring an uninterrupted supply to the mess. He tried to apprise Cdr Bajaj of the ground realities, but to no avail. Vishal became even more frustrated when he heard that the contractor was a friend of Cdr Bajaj and had secured the contract through personal recommendation.

Vishal was under tremendous pressure at work as more time was required for mess activities. Meanwhile, Cdr Sharma had expressed his displeasure that Vishal was wasting time in mess activities and ignoring his primary duties. Vishal tried to convince him of the increased workload in the mess, but Cdr Sharma remained unmoved. He told Vishal that the ATC duties were his primary responsibility and he was not bothered about his secondary duties.

casual attitude

The mess staff included the chef, Ram Singh, two junior cooks and five stewards, besides a few casual workers. Vishal had received several complaints about the chef from his subordinates for not reporting for duty on time, harassing his juniors and smoking in the kitchen. Upon investigation Vishal found that the chef was fairly senior but had missed out on promotions due to his casual attitude, undisciplined behaviour and drinking habits. He warned the man about coming late and smoking habits. Once he found Ram Singh eating lunch in the kitchen despite a rule against this and a separate rest room for the mess staff.

However, there was no change in the chef's behaviour. Vishal warned him on several occasions but with no effect. Once during an inspection of the kitchen at dinner time, Vishal found some dishes were prepared which were not on that day's menu. Upon enquiry, he was informed that Cdr Bajaj had organised a party at home and had ordered the dishes. Vishal called the chef and told him to inform him before doing any such work in the future. He did not feel good about the way things were done at the cost of the other officers' benefit.

When Vishal caught Ram Singh smoking in the kitchen, he was very upset and summoned him to his office. Vishal asked him for a written statement on why he had been smoking in the kitchen despite numerous warnings. Ram Singh refused to do so and replied, 'Sir, I am not going to write any statement. You can take whatever action you want.' This act of indiscipline infuriated Vishal; he immediately called up Cdr Bajaj, but the latter was not available. He drafted an official letter to the regulating officer, the in-charge of the disciplinary department, narrating the incident and requesting him to take appropriate disciplinary action against the chef. A day after the incident, Vishal was summoned by Cdr Bajaj. He found the chef outside the office. Cdr Bajaj enquired about the incident and Vishal narrated the entire episode and added that he had tried to contact him earlier.

complaints received

Cdr Bajaj informed him that he, too, had received several complaints about the chef and would take necessary action himself. He called Ram Singh inside and made him apologise to Vishal. He asked Vishal to withdraw his letter to the disciplinary department. Vishal realised that the entire act was an attempt to hush up the matter unofficially. There was no sincere effort by Cdr Bajaj to punish the errant employee. Vishal was convinced that an apology in the closed confines of his office was not an appropriate solution to flouting of rules in the presence of several people.

He was worried that if the matter was hushed up, it would encourage other mess staff to break rules. Vishal was a highly disciplined officer and valued the implementation of rules. He politely refused to retract his letter. Cdr Bajaj lost his temper and yelled at him. He also blamed Vishal for not informing him before taking action. He warned his junior to remain within his limits and not try to change the functioning of the system.

Vishal left his office dejected. He thought whether all the effort was worth it? Why did he take so much pain to do his work. His senior was not happy, he did not have any time for himself, and the work offered no reward or satisfaction. He was unable to figure out where he had gone wrong.

THE SAGA OF 4P*

It was a gloomy morning. Ishita S. Tyagi dropped off her daughter Misha at school on her way to work. It was past 9 a.m. and she had a meeting with her boss at 9:15 a.m. She could see the bright blue and red 4P banner with its mouth watering pizza snap at a corner of the crossroads. The car's air conditioning failed to cool her as she navigated the traffic. Reaching the office, she raced past the usual morning crowd at the 4P outlet to the boardroom on the second floor. This was one of the most important meetings in her short but highly successful career. She was clear about the available options but had no clear answers.

Ishita's options

Born and brought up in Mumbai in an open-minded environment, Ishita had always been encouraged to express her views and take her own decisions. Educated in a private school, with a good academic record throughout, she was a go-getter. Always ready to explore and experiment, she often took decisions that surprised many. But she usually came up trumps in most of them. She graduated in mathematics honours with distinction. Her final

*Acknowledgements: Alaknanda Ghosh, Dheeraj Renganth, Jit Lahiri and Joypratip Sengupta.

year project 'A mathematical analysis to evaluate the consumer psyche in urban India' had won her accolades. She joined a top management school in Mumbai and specialised in Human Resource Management. Despite several offers, she decided to join 4P that had started its Mumbai operations a year earlier.

4P: the world leader

Founded in 1960, Popeye Pizza Parlour Private Ltd (4P) is the recognised world leader in pizza delivery. It operates a network of company-owned and franchise-owned stores in the United States and abroad. 4P's vision is indicative of a company of exceptional people on a mission to be the best pizza delivery company in the world.

Like many corporate success stories, 4P started out with just one store in 1960. By 1978 there were 200 4P stores, 1,000 by 1983 and 5,000 by 1989. Today it has more than 7,000 stores, including over 2,000 outside the United States.

4P in India

The Rs150 crore pizza industry, growing at an annual rate of 50 per cent, is expanding at a frantic pace. In the wake of economic reforms in India in 1991, the economy began to boom. Taxes were slashed, income levels rose, lifestyles began to change and people began to aspire for international brands.

When 4P entered Mexico, the closest parallel to India, pizza was not the local food. Following its huge success in Mexico, India was automatically seen as the next logical choice for expansion. In India, too, the concept was unfamiliar when 4P opened its first outlet in Delhi. The launch was based on a careful market study which revealed that income levels in the city were growing faster than in any other metro and willingness among customers to experiment was higher. In India pizzas had previously been available only in five-star hotels in Delhi, Mumbai and some parts of Gujarat and Punjab because of NRI connections. The profit margins generated, much higher than what pizza chains in other countries earned, encouraged the company to open outlets all over the country. The company tied up with Hindustan Oil Corporation (HOC) to set up around 100 pizza outlets in the latter's petrol refilling stations in 16 cities.

initial years

Ishita joined 4P as a management trainee and was inducted into the Worli outlet in Mumbai. The organisational policy encouraged new trainees to start from the basic frontline office. Ishita was able to observe and interact with a variety of customers. On her own initiative she would collect data on various aspects like consumer personalities, food preferences and sales patterns across the day. Six months later she was promoted to manager of the Worli outlet.

She adopted several innovative marketing strategies based on the observations that she had made during her training period. She introduced a tollfree concept for ordering pizzas over the telephone. A play zone was earmarked for children at the outlet apart from other promotional activities. A unique policy that she adopted was to customise the menu according to the time of the day which won her the best customer satisfaction 4P outlet award in Maharashtra.

4P followed a policy of standardisation under which all its outlets had a uniform brand identity, with focus on quality, uniformity in product menus and taste across outlets, and strong quality controls. Mr Gupta, the regional head of Maharashtra, encouraged innovative ideas and allowed flexibility in the usual 4P policy for the Worli outlet. In fact, he was very impressed by Ishita's initiatives and encouraged her to experiment with newer strategies.

Ishita married Arjun Tyagi on 12 March 1997. Arjun was the marketing head of a leading FMCG company and led a very hectic life.

new avenues

On 20 August 1998 Ishita was checking the sales figures of the past month when she received a call from Mr Gupta. He had recommended her name as the area sales manager for the new 4P outlet in Ahmedabad. He informed her that the company would appreciate any innovative strategies that she might want to implement to make the Gujarat venture successful.

Ishita was faced with the dilemma of choosing be⁺ween her family and a growing career. Her lack of knowledge of the local environment was also a hindrance. Finally, she decided to take the plunge. She had been with the organisation for only 2 years and hence the move was a big step for her.

The new outlet did not have any distinctive features and was identical to the standard 4P outlets. Not much market research had been done to understand the local lifestyle and preferences. The outlet was located at Stadium Circle, close to CG Road, the commercial and social hub of Ahmedabad. The choice of location was dictated by the large crowds that flocked to CG Road. The target customers of 4P were the 12–30 years age group, which crowded the area in the evenings. The standard menu comprised 18 types each of non-vegetarian and vegetarian pizza toppings with four kinds of pizza bases—thin crust, stuffed crust, pan fried and hand tossed. Also available were a variety of dips and spreads, French fries, garlic bread, and crispy fried chicken wings.

Encouraged by her experience of successful strategies in Mumbai, Ishita decided to adopt the same strategies in Ahmedabad. However, she was surprised when the sales did not increase substantially during the next 5 months. Around this time, the abundant availability of milk at low prices, the huge untapped market, greater economic prosperity and evolving eating habits of the target segment made 4P focus its attention on the Gujarat region. Mr Joshi was appointed as the regional head of Gujarat.

conflict in views

Mr Joshi had worked for 22 years in a reputed food and beverages PSU. He had joined 4P when it began its operations in India as the head of the sales department in Delhi. His experience in a PSU made him a stickler for organisational rules and policies. After joining the Ahmedabad office, he discontinued all the promotional activities initiated by Ishita which led to regular conflicts between them. Forced to be under control, Ishita felt a dip in her confidence level and started questioning the viability of her strategies.

Ishita discussed the issue with Arvind Shah, a friend. While chatting with him she asked him about his preferences for eating in a pure vegetarian restaurant over one serving both vegetarian and non-vegetarian food. Arvind believed in traditional Gujarati values and principles. He said that he would prefer 4P pizzas to be served in a completely vegetarian restaurant. He did not have any specific bias against a non-vegetarian restaurant but personally he was uncomfortable with the practice. For example, many people who did not eat non-vegetarian food felt uneasy at its sight and smell. 'If my friend was sitting next to me and eating a chicken pizza, the smell would make me queasy. And of course, that will kill my appetite to a certain extent.'

Hearing Arvind's views gave Ishita a brainwave. She thought of setting up a completely vegetarian outlet in Ahmedabad, but was sceptical of Mr Joshi's approval of her proposal. She thought of conducting an unofficial market research to validate her idea and she contacted some students in a leading management institute in the city to carry out the research. Conducted over a period of 4 months, the results of the research confirmed her belief in the viability of the proposition. Mr Joshi was initially reluctant to accept the proposal, but in the face of strong support for the idea, he finally gave the go-ahead for the scheme.

grand opening

The location for the new outlet was the premises of Fun Republic, a multiplex in Ahmedabad. Ishita was busy preparing for the grand opening of the outlet when she received a surprise call from Pizza Cottage. Pizza Cottage, another major player in the pizza market, was opeining its first outlet in Gujarat and wanted to recruit Ishita as its regional head. Ishita was so caught up and excited by her new venture that she turned down the offer immediately.

Experimenting with a new marketing approach, 4P began to put emphasis on fast home delivery rather than on the pizza itself. Ishita explained, 'Our pizzas have a major content of flour and cheese. To enjoy these flavours to the fullest, the pizza has to be consumed hot. This basically means that when a customer orders a 4P pizza he should get it while it's still hot. This is our new operating line.' To fulfil this objective, the location was carefully selected. The Fun Republic multiplex had ample parking place for the delivery vehicles and was easily accessible. The other food joints in the building also offered vegetarian fare, which went with 4P's new image. The vegetarian items were retained in the menu and the non-vegetarian dishes were deleted. To add variety to the reduced list, Jain pizza was introduced. This was basically a pizza without any onion or garlic in it. According to the earlier research report, the market for Jain customers was quite large. 4P decided not to advertise this and preferred publicity by word of mouth. As Mr Joshi said, 'Who could be better advertisers than satisfied customers?'

power play

Sales at the outlet were slack for the initial 3 months. People were not very sure about the differences between this particular outlet and the previous one. Some time was required for the message to spread. 4P was highly performance-oriented and did not believe in hierarchy to reward employees who performed well. Mr Joshi realised this and the potential growth in sales at this particular outlet. He was apprehensive that Ishita may pose a threat to his position in the organisation. He managed to convince the top management that Ishita's presence would have a negative impact on their market image. Shortly after this, he called her and told her that 4P had invested so much in her idea, but it was not showing results. Trying to change an established image could affect their growth. The top management had taken this seriously. But given her past record it had decided to be generous and transfer her to 4P's wholly-owned subsidiary in Bangladesh, where it was investing around $2 million.

Ishita was highly surprised and shocked at this response. She had high expectations from the project and maintained that 3 months was too short a time to assess the accurate value of a project. Mr Joshi gave her a day's time to think and let him know her decision by 9:15 a.m. the next day.

Ishita returned to her cabin dejected and broken hearted. She was shaken out of her reverie by the sudden ringing of her phone. It was the HR manager of Pizza Cottage. Her idea had been highly appreciated by them and they wanted her to reconsider her earlier decision. The offer was to join them as the regional head of Gujarat.

5

❖

personal and interpersonal dynamics at work

Expected Learning Outcomes

♦ *Comprehend the framework of how a manager's life gets affected by factors that are internal to the organisation.*

♦ *Identify the way in which the personal and social life of a manager crosses into the organisational systems and affects organisational dynamics.*

Organisation theorists concede that individuals are the unique product of their environment and the responses to the same stimuli vary significantly from one person to another and for the same person at a different time and in a different situation (Furnham, 2000). Most organisations tend to structure organisational arrangements by way of setting a common goal through a universal route of systems, strategies and structure, keeping in mind certain general assumptions about the behaviour of people

(Becker, Huselid and Ulrich, 2001). It is difficult for any organisational system to accommodate or respond to the complexity of human behaviour in the designing of workplace systems in the face of changes in external environmental conditions. Therefore, organisations continue to struggle to maintain a balance between what the organisation expects from people and what people actually desire to do. Some organisations use 'pull and push' mechanisms such as rules and regulations, motivational techniques, and behavioural modification programmes for this purpose. Progressive organisations consider realignment as a continuous need and initiate systematic organisation-wide change management programmes periodically in order to enhance organisational effectiveness. Most of these attempts are intended to reduce personal and interpersonal problems in the organisation as they give rise to pulls and pushes, which can hamper the productivity and performance of individuals in the organisation.

DETERMINANTS OF PERSONAL AND INTERPERSONAL DYNAMICS

Organisational practitioners are increasingly realising the fact that a manager's life on any given day does not begin and end in the office. Each individual manager is influenced not only by the organisational factors, but is also governed by his personal context such as past experiences, and current social and family issues. A manager's responses in the organisation are influenced by three contextual factors:

1. Personal needs that include what he aspires for, his values and attitudes, and past and current personal experiences.
2. His family and social needs as he has to respond to his own priorities toward his spouse, parents, children, friends and other social relationships.
3. Organisation factors such as organisational goals, behavioural conduct with subordinates, superiors and peers, job responsibility and other organisational priorities.

A managerial response is the result of a complex interaction of these three factors. These interactions constitute sources of positive or negative psychological energy, which in turn determines the personal and interpersonal dynamics at work. In order to manage effective personal and interpersonal relations at the workplace, organisational designers have to be sensitive to all the three factors and create adequate space for interaction across these factors in the organisation.

Figure 5.1
Managerial Response as a Result of
Interplay of the Three Life Dimensions

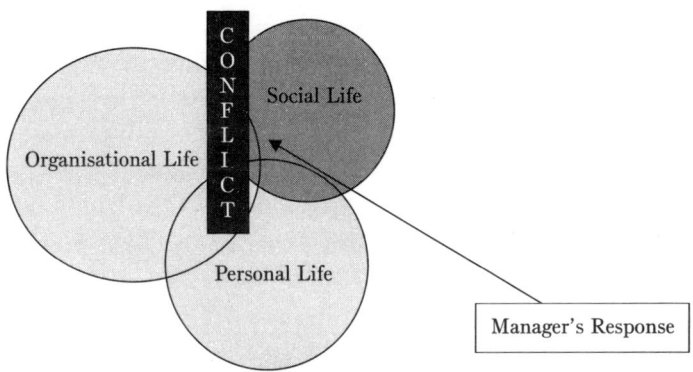

To obtain a holistic perspective of managerial behaviour, it is important to analyse managerial actions and decisions with reference to a wide range of personal, social and organisational variables. This will help in identifying the areas of conflict between personal and organisation needs. This insight will facilitate in developing a synergistic relationship between the individual and the organisation.

ISSUES OF PERSONAL AND INTERPERSONAL DYNAMICS

1. A number of personal and interpersonal conflicts that arise in organisations can be traced to factors outside the

organisation. Managerial behaviour is largely influenced by personal, family and social needs. These include needs, motives and perception of a manager combined with social interventions—demands and support. Therefore, any organisational intervention based on the assumption that a manager exists in isolation of his personal and social environment may be counter-productive. Despite attractive motivational reinforcements, a manager's job commitment and dedication, time management and ability to handle conflicts can be adversely affected by personal and social factors.

2. To satisfy a number of personal and social needs, a manager may adopt a narrow perspective of his job responsibilities which may sometimes work against the interest of the organisation. Driven by personal and social needs, a manager may make work related choices and decisions such as selection of the nature of job assignments, preferences of colleagues, and personal style (authority and power) of handling job situations. A manager's responses to work responsibilities may be influenced by unexpected familial and social expectations and responsibilities.

3. Organisations expect a person to be a complete organisation man and adhere to organisational norms in all possible circumstances. In fact, the complete immersion of a manager into organisational reality is not possible. Organisations do this by imposing stringent rules about work hours, excessive work pressure, creating job insecurity, or changing the location of job or job responsibilities. These interventions cause strain and stress at the personal, social and family levels. For example, excessive work pressure may force a manager to neglect his personal priorities or not give attention to family and social needs. Disturbances in the personal and social life of a manager may have negative consequences for the organisation in terms of poor interpersonal relations at the job, low job effectiveness, etc.

A proper assessment of the likely personal and social constraints that a manager may experience is a precursor to arrangements to create synergistic advantages by integrating the personal and social needs with the needs of the organisation. Many organisations have developed mechanisms to address these issues, for example, flexible working hours, choice of job location, perks and mentoring programmes.

CASES IN PERSONAL AND INTERPERSONAL DYNAMICS

The nine cases presented in this module cover a wide range of personal and interpersonal issues. Of these, five describe how a personal and social need of a manager crosses into the organisational territory and boundary. 'Ambitious' discusses the use of a manager whose ambition led him to take a managerial decision to unduly exploit the client's weakness.

'Shattered Dreams' describes a person working in a call centre whose poor performance led to a number of consumer complaints. The poor performance was due to a series of setbacks—differential treatment by the employer, hardships in the family and chronic sickness resulting from odd working hours.

'Reaching High' describes an individual who was going through an emotionally disturbing phase when he joined the job. Once he recovered from the phase, he found himself hungry for achievement and faster growth in the organisation. He devoted all his time to move up the hierarchy. He got multiple promotions but soon realised that while the company had prospered his scope for growth had narrowed down.

'Choices' and 'A Difference in Perspective' examine how issues in an organisation can crop up on account of a manager's personal and social problems. 'Choices' discusses a well-performing employee whose quality of work suddenly dropped. For a while her immediate superior tried to do all her work, in order to cover up. Subsequently it was found that serious matrimonial problems were affecting her work performance. When the organisation tried to intervene to improve her involvement and productivity, she resigned from the job. The interpersonal relationship between two colleagues is illustrated in 'A Difference in Perspective'. A woman employee misread her male colleague's intentions and proposed marriage to him. As it turned out, he was already married. She finally sued him for sexual harassment.

The other four cases discuss how organisations cross into the personal and social lives of managers. 'Everyone Needs Recognition' presents the internal conflict of an individual because of frequent partiality and indifference of the organisation which affected his personal life. Matters reached an extreme when he finally gave up and decided to go back to his family business despite a strong urge to prove himself independent of family support.

'Full Circle' describes the case of an individual who was frequently transferred from one place to another and across projects. The constant shifts affected his family life and hindered his building up proper competency in any one area. He finally left the job, but not before it had affected his personal life.

The lack of sensitivity of an organisation towards the personal needs and problems of its employees is brought out in 'Trouble in Paradise'. The manager gave his all to the job, including sacrificing his family life. One day when he had to take leave because of an emergency in the family, his boss took stern action against him. The manager was confused as to whether to save the job or leave it to avoid further trouble.

'Shifting Ladders' describes a manager who had been a good performer. His company transferred him to a location which created problems in his personal and family life. He was in a dilemma as to whether to continue with the job or to explore other opportunities.

REFERENCES

Becker, E. Brian, Huselid, Mark A. and Ulrich, Dave. (2001). *The HR scorecard: Linking people, strategy, and performance.* Boston, MA: Harvard Business School Press.

Furnham, A. (2000). Work in 2020: Prognostications about the world of work twenty years into the millennium. *Journal of Management Psychology, 15*(3), 242–254.

CASES ON PERSONAL AND INTERPERSONAL DYNAMICS AT WORK*

key learnings

♦ *Diagnose the cause of interpersonal conflicts that may arise while performing a job.*

♦ *Identify factors causing lack of motivation due to a rigid work culture in an organisation.*

♦ *Comprehend the process of balancing personal aspirations with professional goals.*

♦ *Identify the pressures of family and work in the life of a manager.*

AMBITIOUS

Ajay was a fresh graduate from the Department of Engineering, Jadavpur University. His academic record had been good throughout. After passing from school with flying colours, he took the

Acknowledgements: Abir Kanjilal, Arvind Krishnan, Indranil Das, Nitin Kumar, Ratnakar Mani and Suman Nag.

joint entrance exams of his state and enrolled in the engineering college. He had specialised in electrical engineering. He was a friendly and jovial person. Because of his popularity he had been elected general secretary of the college.

on the job

Ajay was recruited by Samurai Electrical Pvt. Ltd during campus selections. Samurai, a rapidly growing company with an annual turnover of over Rs 60 crore, dealt mainly in heavy electrical equipment. Its clients included industry giants like NTPC, BHEL and SEB. The core business was to repair and rewind high voltage generators, motors and turbines. Given the high-referral for such work, the company preferred annual contracts from its clients. Along with Ajay 12 fresh engineers were recruited from campuses across the state and they were all posted in the testing department.

The workload in the department varied from phase to phase. Whenever a generator or motor had to be repaired, work was hectic. A series of tests were conducted to locate the fault in the machine. Then the equipment was sent to the appropriate department for repairs. After repairs the machine was sent back to the testing department for checking before being delivered to the client. Hence, there was no fixed work schedule for the employees of the department. There were phases when there was hardly any work and they had a lot of free time on hand. Ajay's competence enabled him to complete the allotted work quickly.

widening interests

However, after a few months the relatively slack pace of work diminished his interest level. He was frequently struck by the thought that he was not gaining sufficient insight into the industry and was wasting time. After discussing with some friends he decided to enrol in a management course for which he had to appear for the Common Admissions Test (CAT). He wanted to do postgraduation in marketing. But he did not want to leave his job. As he had enough free time he could put in a few hours of study every day. He did not want his work to suffer either so he divided his time between his job and studies. This caused some resentment among his colleagues who perceived his study as a pretext to shirk work. They even complained to the higher authorities.

Ajay was summoned by his immediate boss, Pranab Roy. By skilfully presenting the facts, he was able to convince his boss of his efficiency and sincerity. In fact, Mr Roy was impressed by his confidence. Gradually, the two developed a good rapport and Mr Roy learnt of Ajay's interest in marketing. Meanwhile Ajay's relationship with some of his peers soured. Being outgoing and friendly by nature, he did not like this cold behaviour.

Mr Roy began to assign small marketing assignments to Ajay who enthusiastically applied himself to the task and obtained good results. He was hopeful that the experience would help him get a better job once he had completed his MBA.

a 'major' problem

One day Arindam Das, the marketing manager, received a phone call from NTPC, an important client of Samurai. One of their central motors had broken down and had to be repaired at the earliest. The defective motor was sent to the testing department and it was found that the problem was not a major one and could be repaired within 10 days. The total cost would be approximately Rs 6 lakh. Mr Das called up Ajay and told him to meet the production manager of NTPC, Sham Sukla and negotiate the deal. Given the importance and urgency NTPC attached to the work, Ajay was asked to quote Rs 10 lakh as the fee.

The next day Ajay met Mr Sukla. During the discussion he learnt that the motor was crucial for NTPC's daily functioning which was probably the reason the officials had overestimated the magnitude of the defect. He decided to capitalise on Mr Sukla's insecurity and take a gamble. He affirmed Mr Sukla's estimate that it was a major problem and would cost Rs 15 lakh for repair. After a brief negotiation an agreement was reached for Rs 14 lakh.

Back in the office Ajay was the centre of attention. The staff members, particularly Mr Das, praised Ajay for his negotiation skills. Mr Roy even announced a monetary reward for him. Ajay invited the entire testing department out for dinner.

But somewhere he still felt cut off by the junior engineers. They tried to avoid him and gave him the cold shoulder. He felt that they were not happy with his action. He realised that if this attitude of his colleagues did not change, he would have a tough time at the workplace. He began to think of his future: his chances of growing within the organisation seemed bright. He thought that after attaining a certain level of seniority he could look for better opportunities elsewhere and he may not even enrol in a MBA programme. On the other hand, the continued antagonism of his colleagues was affecting him negatively.

SHATTERED DREAMS*

It was 7 o'clock in the morning and Amit Bali had just returned after a long night at work, exhausted and yearning to sleep. Amit was an enterprising young man who worked in the call centre of a reputed MNC that had recently started its operations in India. The call centre had been operating from the US earlier. The company had shifted base to India when it realised that this move would cut down overheads to nearly one-eighth of the expenses in the US. Since the centre was for US clients, the work hours had to be scheduled accordingly. Being a relatively new concept in India and offering good job opportunities, the call centre attracted the youth in particular. In its first year of operation the company hired 2,500 people.

*Acknowledgements: Gautam Jain and Mohammad Ahmad.

five bands

Amit was among the first to be recruited in 1996 and had been working ever since. He started with an initial salary of Rs 6,000 a month. The organisation hierarchy is divided into bands. At the bottom is a group of process associates governed by senior customer care executives. Above the executives are process developers. These ranks form Band 5 of the company. Band 4 comprises assistant managers, managers and senior manager. Band 3 includes the operations leader and the assistant vice president. Band 2 includes the vice president and Band 1 the CEO of the company in India.

Growth opportunities for entry level employees also are immense. If an employee performs consistently well then he has a better chance for growth. There is a lot of transparency in the promotion process. An employee who joins at the Band 5 level can reach Band 4 in a span of 2–3 years and Band 3 in 3–4 years. Band 2 would take another 5–6 years. Thus, a Band 5 employee can reach Band 2 within 10–12 years. Performance is the sole criterion for moving up the ladder of success. The salary difference between a Band 5 and a Band 2 employee is such that a person who joins at an annual salary of Rs 72,000 can reach a CTC package of Rs 14 lakh a year.

Amit joined the company as a Band 5 employee, a fresh BCom (Hons) graduate from Lucknow University. His father was a senior clerk at the Faizabad branch of Rajasthan Bank. The youngest in the family, Amit had two elder sisters. During Amit's formative years the family barely had enough money to sustain the family of five and his father had to work hard to make ends meet. After completing his graduation, the next logical step for Amit was to take up a job to supplement his father's meagre income. That was when he shifted to Delhi and joined the call centre industry, which was on the upswing.

corporate ladder

Amit was not only hard working, but also warm-hearted, always willing to stretch himself for his colleagues whenever they had problems. This made him very popular among his fellow workers. He lived alone in a rented apartment and initially had difficulties in managing on his own. Gradually he got over the initial hiccups and oriented himself to life in the city. High on ambition, he devoted himself totally to his work. He realised that the only way to move up the corporate ladder was through hard work and perseverance. His seniors were happy with his work.

Soon he realised that things were not as rosy as they seemed. He began to face problems both at work and back home. Not having prior exposure to such facilities, as computers and internet, he was not technology savvy. Though he tried to be at par with his peers, the lack of formal training in software and systems became a hindrance. Even after 3 months of rigorous training at the call centre, he failed to achieve the required typing speed. His job was to maintain the customer database along with handling calls. The expected speed was 50–60 words per minute, but Amit could only manage 25–30 words despite his best efforts. While he handled the calls very well his poor typing skills pulled down his overall performance. His seniors were very happy with his calls and would have liked to give him the monthly 'customer services' star award', but his poor typing skills proved to be a major drawback.

flexible slab

Things became worse when one day he saw a colleague's monthly salary slip for Rs 14,000. Though they were both in the same position and had joined the company at the same time, his monthly salary was only Rs 9,000. After giving it some thought Amit realised that 2 years ago the company had changed its employment policies following which the salary was structured on a flexible slab rate wherein an employee was paid in accordance with the amount and quality of work that he did and how much business he generated for the company. The difference in salaries troubled Amit.

personal issues

This also brought other personal issues to the fore. Every month he sent at least Rs 3,000 to his family. His father was to retire in a year's time and both his sisters had to be married which increased Amit's financial responsibility. As his father's savings were not enough to meet these expenses he had been under pressure to send more money. His company provided a maximum personal loan of Rs 75,000 to Band 5 employees at 0 per cent interest, to be repaid within 4 years. However, this amount too would not have met the requirement. Amit was also of marriageable age and would soon be expected to settle down in life.

chronic problems

Working night shifts at the call centre was telling on his health. His working hours were from 8 p.m. till 5 a.m. and every day he had to commute for almost 4 hours. He left his house around 6 o'clock in the evening and was back only around 7 o'clock the next morning. Also, given his generous nature he ended up spending a lot of time helping his colleagues handle their work. All these added to his woes and his health was affected. Continuous sitting and working on a computer led to chronic backache and eyesight problems.

The company policy prohibited him from discussing his salary structure with any other staff member. His personal problems coupled with the differential treatment at the workplace upset him. He was unable to concentrate on the work at hand. As a result his work suffered; the number of complaints from customers increased and the management had to spend a lot of time placating irate clients.

Since he was known to be a diligent worker, no immediate action was taken against him. But from Amit's perspective something had to be done. Familial pressures were increasing and he was not sure how long he could carry on. That morning as he lay on his bed he wondered about the future.

REACHING HIGH*

Mridul was happy, he had been promoted to marketing manager of United Electricals Pvt. Ltd. He was the youngest and least experienced of the staff members, just beginning to gain ground in his work. This promotion was an opportunity for him to consolidate his position in the company. Had someone told him a year ago that he would be successful, he would have never believed it.

Coming from a middle class family, Mridul was an emotional person, easily affected by even minor incidents. His analytical skills were very good and he aspired to join the Indian Civil Services. However, twice he had been called for the interview but was not able to clear it. Around the time of his third attempt, his mother went through two complicated surgeries. The treatment and aftercare were not only time consuming but also put a heavy financial burden on the family. This was compounded by the death of his closest friend in a car accident. Overcome and pressurised by these traumatic experiences, Mridul could not prepare properly for the exam and failed again.

Disillusioned, he joined United Electricals as a sales executive at the age of 24. The company manufactured various electrical equipment. As the company had several clients in the mining industry, Mridul's grounding in geology stood him in good stead. He was part of a four-member team. The other members were far

*Acknowledgements: Mrinal Braj, Mudit Singhal, Neha Joshi, Ninad P. Raikar and Viniti Chandiramani.

more experienced than him and had a degree in Sales Management: one of them had been with the company for 10 years, another for 5 years and the third for 2 years.

The initial period was difficult as Mridul had not yet recovered from the twin tragedies. Besides, he had difficulty adjusting to his colleagues. Though he was in the same position as others, because of his relative inexperience he had to do all the ground work. The only saving factor was that his boss, Animesh Sinha, the marketing manager who reported directly to the proprietor, was cooperative and understanding.

handling clients

Within a few months he had got the feel of things. He was given charge of clients from the mining industry. His superior knowledge and sober nature earned him their respect. His perspicacity led him to discover that one of the imported equipment used in the field could be useful in preventing short circuits in coal mines, where the high probability of methane gas leakage, combined with electrical discharge, increased the chances of a fatal explosion. He discussed this with Mr Sinha as a market opportunity for the company to start manufacturing the equipment indigenously. Mr Sinha, however, was not fully convinced of the feasibility.

Within a period of around 10 months Mridul was achieving his targets successfully, but he did not experience a sense of satisfaction. His craving for achievement and continued emotional anchoring in past traumas prevented him from enjoying the comfortable work position he held.

moving up

Mr Sinha had received feelers from another company that wanted an experienced person to handle its marketing department. After contemplating the proposition for several months, he decided to accept the offer. This created a vacancy in United Electricals.

The proprietor, Mr Dhawan, had two options—either to recruit an MBA graduate at a higher salary or promote someone in-house, from the sales executives. He had observed Mridul's sincerity and commitment to work and after much consideration he decided to promote Mridul to the post.

This was a pleasant surprise for Mridul. So far only MBAs had been appointed to similar posts. It was a great opportunity for him to grow and break away from his personal turmoil. Mr Dhawan's confidence in him was a moral booster. But the road ahead was not easy. Those who had once been his colleagues became his subordinates. They expressed their concern at someone so young and inexperienced being appointed to the high post. He had lacked their support even as a colleague; being able to make them work under him posed a bigger challenge.

problems at work

Satish, 38, was the senior-most person in the sales force. With 10 years of work experience, he knew the job well and commanded respect in the department. He was not too ambitious and was happy with his comfortable lifestyle. Mridul took great care in dealing with him and always sought his advice in functional matters. This approach worked and soon he found a good friend in Satish.

One person who had a serious problem with Mridul was Ramesh who had 5 years of work experience. He made no effort to hide his resentment about the decision. He did not report to Mridul regularly and was rude whenever he was questioned. He opposed even the routine decisions taken within the department. Mridul was aware of the reason behind Ramesh's hostility, but was taken aback by its intensity. He tried to discuss it with Ramesh, but with no success.

The new sales executive who replaced Mridul was Munda. He was hired under some political pressure and was not qualified for the post as revealed by his performance. He would arrive in the office drunk and use his political clout to shirk work. Being a small company, United Electricals could not afford to support such non-performing employees for long. The sales figures were also getting affected. Despite several warnings and even a cut in his salary, Munda did not improve his performance. Finally, he was fired.

However, Munda filed a case against the company in the Scheduled Tribe Commission and labour court, accusing it of discrimination. He stated that he was fired because he belonged to the ST category and there was no other valid reason for the action. After dragging the case for a while, the court finally decided in favour of Munda. United Electricals was asked to pay Rs 25,000 as compensation to him. Though there was nothing he could have done about it, Mridul held himself morally responsible for the incident.

expanding horizons

Mridul was confident that the company would grow faster if it manufactured the equipment required in the mining industry. The difficulty was in convincing the production manager and Mr Dhawan to go along with his idea and invest in the development of the equipment. However, his persistence and Mr Dhawan's faith in him paid off. Investment was made in research and development and in about a year's time the product was ready. The cost was almost one-fourth that of a similar imported machine and it was cheaper. Field trials showed the equipment to be satisfactory. Industry demand for the equipment soon increased and the company's annual turnover rose significantly.

Meanwhile, the state was divided by the central government. United Electricals faced a peculiar problem relating to its transactions with the state electricity boards. The company's dues, running into lakhs of rupees, remained unpaid because of non-division of assets between the two state electricity boards. Mridul solved this problem innovatively by subcontracting work to small contractors, thus minimising the company's need for working capital. The company could fulfil its work obligations with a reduced labour force and without taking large loans.

In another instance the state electricity board issued a tender for some machinery required for rural electrification. Some corrupt officials in the Ministry for Power wanted money from the board to pass specific tenders. The board in turn wanted money from the companies bidding for the tender. To profit from the contract the companies had to compromise on the quality of the electrical equipment. In a meeting with Mr Dhawan and the production manager Mridul insisted that they should not compromise in quality. His advice was heeded and quotations were given as per standard practices, but United Electricals lost the contract.

time to move on

His hard work in the marketing department resulted in a 15 per cent growth for the company. However, after 2 years Mridul felt that he was stagnating and had reached a plateau in his career. Getting a similar job profile and higher pay package in another company was difficult without an MBA degree. He remembered the famous saying, 'If you do what you've always done, you'll get what you've always got!' He knew that if he wanted a change he should not wait for it to happen; he had to do something himself. It was time to move on.

CHOICES*

It was a usual Monday morning in STC's main office in Hyderabad and the lobby of the marketing and sales firm was abuzz with the chatter of employees catching up on weekend news. As Arpita entered through the glass doors, she looked around her new office.

*Acknowledgements: Atul Rohan Garg, Deepak Singh, Garima, Rashmi Wadhwa and Traptika Chauhan.

She had recently joined as manager, marketing. After completing her MBA (marketing) from a premier management school in Mumbai, she had worked for 6 years with various firms before joining STG.

managing the staff

Her predecessor had left the job around 6 months ago and since then the position had been lying vacant. During that period Varun, senior manager, sales and marketing, was handling the work. He was her immediate boss. Varun reported to the vice president of the company, who in turn was accountable to the CEO. In her capacity as manager Arpita had a team of six assistant managers reporting to her.

She observed that the performance of one of the assistant managers, Sakshi, was not satisfactory. She would frequently fail to meet her deadlines or turn in shoddy or hurriedly completed work. Arpita observed her for a while before taking any action. Talking to Sakshi had no effect. Her increasingly lackadaisical attitude affected the department's productivity.

Arpita thought of reporting the matter to Varun, but was unsure of how he would respond. The fact that Sakshi was popular in the department and had no past records of complaints against her during her 2-year tenure made Arpita all the more hesitant. She tried to cover up the matter by handling Sakshi's work herself. She worked extra hours, sometimes skipping her weekly holidays. This took its toll on her health. But she refrained from reporting the matter as she was apprehensive of creating an unfavourable impression about herself in the new organisation.

annual appraisal

This continued for 4 months till the annual appraisal. Then Arpita decided to take action and reported the matter to Varun. He was surprised that Arpita had not thought it right to report

136 ❖ Shaping Organisational Strategies
such a serious matter earlier. It struck him as odd that Sakshi, who had a good track record, could be so careless with her work. Vaun directed Arpita to take a tougher stand. Perhaps talking to Sakshi directly about how her attitude had affected the department and giving her strict deadlines could help.

Arpita reminded Sakshi regularly of her deadlines, but could not take a strong stand and talk with her openly about the problems she was creating for the department. Though Sakshi began to meet deadlines, the quality of her work continued to be substandard. When Varun asked Arpita about Sakshi's progress, she informed him that there was hardly any change.

Varun decided to confront Sakshi but before that Arpita and he examined the past records. They found that till a year ago Sakshi had received very good performance reports. She had taken a break of 6 months for her marriage. When she returned, the manager's post had become vacant and she did not have any direct authority to report to. Arpita had heard from the office grapevine that Sakshi was not happy with her marriage. She often mentioned taking a break and visiting her maternal home. Also, her new home was very far from the office and much time was spent commuting to and from work. Pending work at home also kept her preoccupied and affected her timings.

drastic step

Realising that her personal life was affecting her work performance, Varun and Arpita called Sakshi for a talk. The latter was surprised to hear that her work was unsatisfactory. No one had told her that directly. She insisted that she was doing her work well.

Both her seniors set down guidelines for her and monitored her work. She made an effort and her work began to improve. After about 2 months of continuing like this, much to everyone's surprise Sakshi resigned from her job. The only official or personal explanation that she gave was that she wanted to do something else in life.

The last anyone heard of Sakshi, she had shifted to Mumbai and had opened a shop selling antiques there.

A Difference in Perspective*

Pradeep Kumar graduated from a reputed management college in Ahmedabad and was immediately recruited by Templeton Worldwide, a leading Delhi-based consultancy. He joined as a programmer-cum-analyst and his responsibilities included design and development of financial software for sales, trading, order execution, etc. He was initially required to work on global software development and support projects. He justified his handsome pay package by his sincere and efficient work. He was promoted to the level of an associate within 3 years of his joining (See Appendix 5.1). Around this time, he got married to a girl of his parents' choice.

family responsibilities

The couple lived in a joint family with Pradeep's parents, his uncle and his family. His wife was a teller in a bank and worked from 10 a.m. to 8 p.m. They managed to spend time with each other only on Sundays. Two years into the marriage they decided to have a child. Soon they were blessed with a daughter and Pradeep was overjoyed. However, work pressure prevented him from spending adequate time with his daughter. His wife had also been promoted to cash authoriser and had additional responsibilities at work. A supportive family system helped them to maintain a balance between home and career. At 35 years of age, he was content with the way things had worked out.

*Acknowledgements: Anuja Chachra, Madhurim Gupta, Sunandini Pande and Tahira Nath.

The same year Pradeep received a salary hike. A promotion in the near future was also likely. He had been with the organisation for 8 years and was popular with his colleagues and subordinates. He headed a team of 15 high-performing analysts, the members shared an informal interaction pattern. They would often go out in the evening after office. The relationship was not so much on a personal level as that of professional camaraderie.

company profile

Templeton Worldwide, a multinational company, is one of the leading financial firms in the world. It deals with investment banking, with the focus on corporate finance, capital raising and advisory work for Indian corporations in both international and domestic capital markets. The company engages in institutional equity sales and trading, supported by research, for both Indian and FII (foreign institutional investors) clients. It also has a presence in the retail distribution and fixed income securities business in India. The company has offices in eight cities in India—Mumbai, Delhi, Kolkata, Chennai, Pune, Bangalore, Hyderabad and Ahmedabad.

While at the lower levels there are a large number of employees, the higher levels have fewer posts. The MD of the Delhi division supervised 300 employees. Employees at each level enjoy much independence and are responsible for individual assignments. The organisation is output-driven and deadlines are strictly adhered to. Meeting clients' standards of expectations is the general practice. The work atmosphere is friendly and informal.

miscommunication at work

Pradeep was on first name terms with his team members. One day he mailed to one of his juniors, Rohini, about some developments in the project they were working on. He also wanted her to call the client to confirm certain details. She mailed back to clarify some doubts she had about the project. This led to a regular exchange of mails where the topics ranged from official communication to jokes and personal issues. They started meeting outside office and developed a close, friendly relationship.

Rohini was 28 years old and single. She had been with Templeton Worldwide for 3 years and had been in Pradeep's team since the beginning. She lived with her parents and had had joined the firm immediately after her postgraduation. However, she misread her relationship with Pradeep. For him, she was just a good friend, but she perceived his intentions as romantic. After 6 months of interaction she approached him and proposed marriage. Pradeep was taken aback at the absurdity of the situation. He informed her that he was already married and never had any such intentions with regard to her.

repercussions

After this interaction Rohini went into depression and her performance was affected. She even became hostile towards Pradeep and the whole team to the extent of bad-mouthing the company within and outside the organisation. This created much discomfort in the work atmosphere. One day Rohini called up Pradeep and threatened to kill herself. Matters worsened when her father intervened and reported a case of sexual harassment to the police. It was at this juncture that the company asked Pradeep to take paid leave until the investigation was completed.

the aftermath

Pradeep lost the support of his subordinates. Many of his friends who heard of the incident stopped talking to him. However, his wife and family stood by him through the turmoil. His wife would accompany him to the court and the police station till the matter was settled. Pradeep asserted that there was no sexual involvement or harassment. The two had interacted by mutual consent and there was no force involved. After a harrowing phase the case against him was dropped due to lack of evidence. A long deliberation by the board was followed by his reinstatement in the organisation. However, the very next day Rohini submitted her resignation letter.

Appendix 5.1: The Organisational Hierarchy at Templeton Worldwide Limited

Managing Director (MD)
Executive Director (ED)
Vice President (VP)
Associate
Analyst
Programmer

Everyone Needs Recognition*

Dreams, ambitions and plans were the driving force behind Rahul Rai's existence. He had topped the class throughout his academic career. Extra-curricular activities and enjoyment were secondary to success in life.

Rahul's father was a businessman dealing in computer software. His other son, Rajesh, helped him in the business. Being brought up in a joint family had its disadvantages. The brothers were always compared with their cousins who were around the same age. Rajesh's cousin Varun was also in the business of computers and was doing better than Rajesh; a fact he did not bother to hide. Whenever he offered to help Rajesh, he made sure that his offer was well publicised.

*Acknowledgements: Mrinal Braj, Mudit Singhal, Neha Joshi, Ninad P. Raikar and Viniti Chandiramani.

Rahul was studying engineering. During final placements his preferred company visited the campus for recruitment. He had always wanted to work for this company and had spent long nights preparing for the interview. The company was engaged in software development and was renowned all over the world in the IT consultancy services sector. His efforts paid off and along with 30 other students he received an offer to join the company as an associate systems engineer.

After 2 months of training he was required to sign an employment bond for 2 years. If he resigned during this period he was expected to pay a training compensation of Rs 2 lakh to the company. As this was his dream job, Rahul did not think twice about the repercussions of such a contract. On completion of his studies, he joined the training programme.

He certainly was happy! He was working for a company he had always admired, with colleagues who were college friends and soon he could ask for a transfer to his hometown—Delhi. At the end of the training period, a performance appraisal was done but, Rahul did not fare as well as he had expected to in spite of his good performance. He was surprised because he had put in extra effort and longer hours as compared to others. However, he chose to let it pass.

choice of location

The new employees were asked to fill in their location preference in the employment form. The choices given were Mumbai, Delhi, Kolkata, Bangalore, Hyderabad and Chennai. Rahul opted for Delhi as he wanted to be closer to home and to his father's business. Strangely, everybody apart from him got the location of his or her choice. He was posted to Mumbai, a city he did not much care for.

He thought it best to directly question the HR department about this decision. The HR manager was not very convincing, she said that since all the vacancies in Delhi had been filled he had to go to Mumbai. No reason was given as to why he alone was denied a posting of his choice.

When he informed his father of the posting the older man advised him to quit the job and join his brother. He wanted his son to be closer home. Rahul understood his father's sentiments but did not want to quit. He had worked hard for it and wanted to prove to the world that he was capable of chalking out his own future. If he joined his brother at that point all the years of hard work would go waste.

His initial enthusiasm dampened, Rahul packed his bags for Mumbai. He was a sensible young man and he knew that if he allowed these petty thoughts to affect him he would not be able move ahead in his career. All he had to do was work sincerely and he would certainly get noticed. Once he got the recognition, he could ask for a transfer to Delhi.

ground realities

As soon as he arrived in Mumbai he headed for the office. The office was elegant and polished—a place that he was proud to be associated with. It was a three-storeyed, centrally air-conditioned building. Swipe cards were issued to employees to enter the building and different department areas. His cabin was on the second floor which he shared with three of his college mates.

Rahul found the projects very interesting and worked wholeheartedly and diligently. The work required software coding skills, part of which he was familiar with. For others, he had to refer to coding manuals.

His initial learning was substantial but after some time the work became repetitive. Each project was only slightly different from the other. He had to do the same coding task everyday. Slowly, the passion ebbed. It seemed his employers were not interested in providing him more challenging work. He had reached the point of saturation. This continued for 10 months. Having completed a year in the organisation (including 2 months spent in training), he was looking for professional growth. Sometimes he was asked to work on technologies that he thought were not at all relevant to the task and was uncomfortable with them. However, hoping for an improvement in the future, he did the work without complaining. Some of his colleagues would laugh at him. One of them, Satish, even remarked, 'Why do you work so hard? They are only using you. They are never going to give you what you deserve. This is called exploitation of labour!' Rahul grimly wished for things to change.

in a rut

That night he did not sleep till late. He knew that his life was stagnating. He did not want to quit and feel like a loser. However he could do something and that was get an MBA degree from a reputed college, either in India or abroad.

Four or five months later another disappointment was in store for him. Some of his colleagues were sent to the US to work on a project for a couple of months. This would give them exposure to a newer and more challenging business environment while he was restricted to the same technical work, sitting in the same cubicle with the same bosses. The only thing that changed was the work pressure. He not only had to work longer hours, but also had to report on Saturdays and Sundays. He received neither any appreciation nor any bonus.

By now he had lost faith in justice and impartiality. He was frustrated. There was so much he wanted to do and was capable of doing, but no one seemed to notice. How could he perform if he was not given any incentive or motivation? His peers had got recognition for similar work. Things were no better at home. Often he would be irritable and rude when he spoke to his family over the phone. His father suggested that if he was not happy with the job he should return home and join his brother. Rahul felt more defeated than ever; he did not know what to do. He waited for dawn.

FULL CIRCLE*

Life had come a full circle for Nishit Trivedi. Sitting in his office at closing time, he glanced at the nameplate on his desk, which read 'Regional Manager, Pathfinder Education Services.' He heaved a sigh of relief and thought that he had been associated with Pathfinder for one and a half years and not a day had passed when he had not given his best to the organisation. He had joined as a centre in-charge at Allahabad and had been promoted to this post within a short span of time. It had been stressful but rewarding. As the voices outside began to fade, Nishit saw his life flash before his eyes.

against the instincts

Nishit had been a good student throughout and been particularly interested in humanities. He wanted to pursue a career in a people-oriented field, but his parents did not approve. They believed that a good student like him should opt for physical sciences, even though both of them were from an Arts background and were in the Central Administrative Services. He gave in to their wishes but because of his lack of interest in the subject, he could not live up to their expectations. However, this proved to be a turning point in his life and made him put in extra effort to prepare for the engineering entrance examinations. He joined an engineering college in Dhanbad and graduated in petroleum engineering. After this he enrolled in a MBA course from a renowned business school in Jamshedpur, but because of his father's untimely demise and subsequent financial constraints he was not able to join the institute.

He eventually joined Gas India (GI), a PSU, as an assistant engineer. He was assigned to the Hajira-Jagdishpur pipeline project. He was unhappy with the work culture, the shift system did

*Acknowledgements: Ritza Trivedi, Saraswati Swamy, Suchi Srivastava and Varun Oberoi.

not suit his biological clock and his performance at the workplace dipped. He expressed his desire for a change in his shift timings but the company refused. This adversely affected him.

Meanwhile his mother began to put pressure on him to get married. Nishit was initially reluctant as he thought that it would distract him from his work. He wanted to be financially secure before he got married. Eventually he gave in to his mother's wishes and married Mansi in a simple ceremony. The marriage was solemnised within a week of Nishit's acquiescence as he had to leave on a month-long official tour to Jamnagar soon after and there were no auspicious dates after that in the near future.

management beckons

Two days after returning from Jamnagar, he was posted to Selari, a small village in Gujarat and 23 miles from the nearest town. He left his wife at her parents' place. Life at Selari was very boring, to pass time he and a senior did a lot of reading and engaged in other academic pursuits. During this time he planned to pursue a degree in management. After 2 years in service he quit his job, one of the highest paid in the sector, and enrolled in one of the premier business schools in India. After specialising in marketing he joined Indraprastha Motors, a private sector automobile company.

At the time the company was going through a rough patch. The life of its once successful models had reached the end. The company considered going back to the drawing board to design models more in sync with the current requirements. This was the company's last attempt at making a comeback as an automobile major. It had put in all efforts and resources into the project which was code named Aquarius.

Nishit was part of the team that had been formed to work with an international consulting firm hired to implement the project. He was very excited about the project and prepared well in advance before the brainstorming sessions. Unfortunately, he met stiff resistance at the meetings. Since he was working with the consultant, he was perceived to be an insider working for an outside company. Though his suggestions were logical, his blunt and frank way of expressing them led him into arguments with even the chairperson of the company. Such conflicts with his seniors only increased with time and he often found himself without a clear project for considerable periods of time. This marked the beginning of his discontent with the company and his job.

at loggerheads

Nishit was constantly transferred from one project to another. As a result, while he was able to develop some good relationships in the organisation, he had no chance to mend the relationships that had gone sour. He felt that the constant transfer was intentional because of his habit of speaking up before his seniors. His work required him to form his own team for implementing the suggestions made by the consultants. Not many people in the organisation took kindly to being ordered about by one of their peers. Besides the transfer across projects, there was a constant change in the nature of work allotted to him. Sometimes he was asked to deal with foreign suppliers, at other times with domestic ones. This diluted his credence as a project developer and his role in general management became unclear.

At that time he became aware of the bureaucratic system prevalent in the organisation. The seniors delegated a lot of their personal work to subordinates. On his last assignment, his senior, who was about to retire, took more interest in investing in the stock market than in doing official work. Though the two shared a good personal rapport, the man's work attitude contrasted with Nishit's standards of professionalism.

On the home front, things were not smooth sailing either. Mansi often complained that he did not spend enough time with her. Nishit realised this, but his work did not permit him any leisure time. He suggested that she should take up a job to keep herself occupied. Mansi, a qualified engineer herself, reacted enthusiastically to the suggestion and took up a job in a new company located in the suburbs.

However, this did not end their problems but only aggravated them. Mansi did well in her job and was soon promoted to project leader. As the unit was located at a distance, she often returned home late. Nishit could not accept this and objected to her late hours. He strongly believed that Mansi should leave her job as it was affecting their family life. Mansi, however, loved her work and refused to quit.

slump in industry

Meanwhile, there were changes not only in the automobile industry, but also in the organisation. There was a slump in the industry. A workers' strike broke out in the company and the rate of attrition was high. The MBAs in the organisation, who were at the middle and top levels, were pampered at the cost of the non-MBA middle and implementation level employees, who actually had more technical knowledge of the automobile industry. This led to a conflict between the groups at the inter- and intra-organisational levels and affected overall productivity.

During his tenure at Indraprastha Motors Nishit had been project guide to several summer interns from business schools. One of his trainees won the first prize at a business meet. This rekindled Nishit's long forgotten interest in the field of knowledge management. This desire, coupled with his growing discontent with the organisation, gave him enough reason to quit his job and look for avenues in knowledge management.

great performance

Six months later Nishit finally joined Pathfinder Educational Services as centre in-charge. Since this meant shifting to Allahabad, Mansi left her job at B&M to accompany him. Due to his excellent performance he was promoted to regional manager (eastern UP). He introduced several innovative initiatives. Immediately after joining, he instilled professionalism into the organisation. The employees were more academically inclined than business-oriented. Nishit trained them to run the enterprise more professionally. After assuming the post of regional manager, he created an in-house design department that handled all the local publicity and promotional activities of the company. This not only reduced its dependence on advertising agencies, but also resulted in cost reduction, thereby increasing the profits. All these activities brought him much respect and recognition. He was suitably rewarded with promotions. He had given his all to the organisation and both of them were growing.

how times change

Shaking himself out of his reverie Nishit smiled as he thought of his 'growth'. His rise at Pathfinder was phenomenal. But had he been slow in achieving success? How different would his life have been had he answered his calling and not given in to parental pressure? What if he would have handled stress better and controlled his impetuous behaviour? Or, was it because of all these that he was where he was now? Were 8 years of his professional life before he joined Pathfinder a waste? Had he been unfair to his wife? Had he lost something personal in his quest for professional success?

TROUBLE IN PARADISE*

Ashwin woke up early with a lump in his throat. He had not been sleeping well since the past several nights and had a throbbing headache. Taking care not to disturb his wife, he got out of bed.

*Acknowledgements: Prashant Jain, Saunak Ghosh, Shitij Jain and Vandana Mehra.

After a quick wash he left for his usual morning jog. Ashwin thought of the day that lay before him and how it would turn out. After all, not every employee was served a show cause notice by the DGM. If he came out of it unscathed it would definitely be a miracle. Not for nothing was Mr Mann called 'Hitler' in work circles. He felt betrayed and hurt. What had he done to deserve this?

flashback

He had started his career as a clerk in a prestigious bank. He was an eager worker, and was liked by his peers. His poor family background did not prevent him from aiming high. His moment of pride came when he was promoted to the rank of officer. Since the beginning he left a mark. His hard work and affability brought him promotions and recognition.

A variety of assignments came his way. He had been the manager of a new rural bank set up in the late 1980s, where he had set up the bank's operations and brought in new business. He was felicitated by the District Collector for his commendable work. He had also been in charge of the foreign exchange division of the Mumbai branch. Ashwin had served as the administrative secretary to the DGM at the head office (south zone). During his tenure he had developed a good rapport with several top officials.

growth in profitability

As the manager of the Ahmedabad branch, he had to work extra hours as there was a policy of a seven-day week. He was entitled to a weekly off, but he usually worked seven days as he believed that it was his responsibility to oversee each day's work. The branch had been performing well under him and the year 2002 saw a 68 per cent growth in deposits and 54 per cent growth in overall profitability.

All this left little time for his family. He would return home tired around 9 p.m. and just crash into bed. His wife never complained, but Ashwin felt guilty at not spending enough time with her. He could not remember the last time they had been out for dinner.

emergency

In April 2003, shortly after the audit had ended and the pressure had eased somewhat, Ashwin reached home to find his wife in tears. His father-in-law, Mr Gupta, had not been keeping well and had been diagnosed as suffering from brain tumour. As malignancy had not been ruled out, he had to be operated upon at the earliest. The best facilities were available only at Chennai. The dilemma was who would accompany him to Chennai. Ashwin being the closest and eldest male relative offered to go with him. He made travel arrangements for the two of them and his young brother-in-law. He also applied for leave from office. The DGM, Mr Mann, was away in Jaipur when Ashwin called. So, he spoke to his secretary, Prashant, whom he had known since his days in Mumbai. They had worked together and shared a good personal relationship. Prashant assured him that he would inform Mr Mann when the latter returned. To be on the safe side, Ashwin faxed his leave application to Mr Mann's office.

operation scheduled

Four days after they reached Chennai, Mr Gupta got an appointment with the doctor. The operation was scheduled for three days later. Things were proceeding smoothly but Ashwin was uncomfortable about being away from work for so long. The doctor was optimistic about Mr Gupta's progress. After a gruelling 5-hour operation, the doctor declared that the operation was successful. Hearing this, Ashwin called up home to inform his wife. She told him that there had been several calls for him from the DGM's office and he had been asked to contact Mr Mann immediately.

Thinking that something was amiss while he was on leave, Ashwin called up the head office and was connected to Mr Mann. He was in for a shock. Mann shouted at him over the phone and accused him of being absent for a prolonged period without taking leave or seeking permission. As much as Ashwin tried to explain his position, or tell him that he had submitted his application for leave, Mr Mann refused to listen to reason. He directed Ashwin to return to Ahmedabad immediately.

boss's wrath

Ashwin rushed to the hospital to discuss Mr Gupta's discharge date with the doctor. He finally met the doctor after waiting for 3 hours. But the doctor recommended keeping Mr Gupta under observation for at least a week before discharging him. Ashwin was in a fix, he could neither leave the old man with his young brother-in-law nor could he stay back any longer and incur his boss's wrath.

After a sleepless night he thought that it would be wrong to leave the patient. He would explain his predicament to Mr Mann and try to convince him that in the present circumstances it was impossible for him to return. He hoped that his boss would be sensitive enough to understand his problem and grant him the leave which was anyway long overdue. But Ashwin was proved wrong later that day when he spoke to his boss.

Ashwin: Good morning, Sir, how are you?

Mr Mann: Cut the crap. When are you getting back?

Ashwin: Sir, please try to understand. My father-in-law has just had an operation for brain tumour and he has to stay in hospital for at least seven more days. I am the only one here with him and so can't leave him alone.

Mr Mann: I don't believe you. You have lied to me once before about sending your leave application and informing Prashant, which he confirms isn't true. I think you are bluffing again and trying to save your skin.

Ashwin: What do you mean? (Voice rising) I have positively informed Prashant. Sir, I am sure there is some misunderstanding.
Mr Mann: I am clear as to what you are trying to do. Do not bluff
any more. Do what you feel, but be ready to face an enquiry
whenever you decide to come back.
Ashwin: But, Sir. But.... Please, give me a chance to explain myself.
Mr Mann: You will get your chance. (Hangs up).

Ashwin felt thoroughly let down as he walked back to the hotel.
Surely he had told Prashant to inform Mr Mann. He may have
forgotten to do so earlier, but why was he lying now? Could he
not understand that he could get Ashwin into trouble by lying?
What baffled him was that his fax also never reached Mr Mann.
However, one thing was certain that he was in trouble. How to
get out of it was the question.

The only positive development was that Mr Gupta recuperated
rapidly and was discharged on the scheduled date. As soon as they
returned to Ahmedabad, Ashwin rushed to the office. Seeing the
faces of his staff members, he realised that something was wrong.
After talking to them he found that in his absence, Mr Mann had
ordered a probe into the functioning of the office by two colleagues
of his from other branches in the city. They had looked into his
personal files and papers.

vindictive stand

Ashwin was thoroughly disgusted for being humiliated in front
of his staff. He seriously considered confronting Mr Mann and
giving him a piece of his mind. Then he thought of discussing
the matter with his previous boss, Sanjeev, who was at the same
level as per Mann. He called up Sanjeev immediately, after hearing
the entire story Sanjeev convinced him not to take any drastic
step. He advised Ashwin to keep his cool and not anger Mr Mann
any further.

This suggestion did not help Ashwin either. Three days passed
before he was able to meet the DGM. There was more bad news:
he was informed that he was being served a show cause notice.

His case would be taken up with the higher authorities and Mr Mann was determined to take stern action as a lesson to others. All Ashwin's pleas went in vain. He even thought of quitting his job. All those years of loyal service, felicitations, good relations with colleagues seemed to have been wiped out in one stroke. Why was Mr Mann so critical of him? The matter was not very serious: even a mild reprimand would have sufficed. A show cause notice would cast serious aspersions on his future growth. Prashant's betrayal also hurt. Was he jealous of Ashwin? Was there any other reason?

Ashwin was in deep trouble. What should be his course of action so as to tackle this problem efficiently? He had still 10 years ahead of him. How could he get out of the mess crisis without antagonising his boss further and securing his future as well?

Shifting Ladders*

Ashish Sengupta obtained a B.Tech. in metallurgical engineering from IIT, Kharagpur in 1985. He was a bright student and a keen sportsperson. He had varied interests, ranging from music, especially western classical, to travelling.

good opportunities

He was recruited by Indica Steel Limited (ISL) during campus placements for its marketing division. After a 5-month training at its Kubera Steel Plant, Ashish was posted in Mumbai as a management trainee. He had initially joined ISL because of job security associated with a public sector company. The prospects for growth as well as work satisfaction in the organisation strengthened his belief that he had made the right choice.

*Acknowledgements: Bindu Thomas, Kartikeya Varma and Neha Dilipkumar.

A decade later, he was happy with his life situation. After 3 years he had been transferred to Ahmedabad for 2 years. Following his marriage he had been transferred back to Mumbai as Assistant Branch Manager. He had a comfortable flat at Andheri, where he lived with his wife and a 6-year-old son. He loved the city and the opportunities it offered. Everything was so convenient and easy to get. As many of his relatives and friends were also in Mumbai, he could get help whenever the need arose.

Ashish had met his wife, Konkona, at IIT where they were studying together. Though an engineer by training, she had chosen to do what she enjoyed more—theatre. She was actively involved in theatre in Mumbai and occasionally held drama workshops and did freelance work for a few schools. She had maintained a balance between her interests and her responsibilities as a wife and mother. Ashish was usually busy at work. Though he was far better off than many of his friends in the private sector, he could not completely discount the pressure of running such a large organisation (see appendix 5.2). He had no time to pursue his earlier hobbies and the family rarely went out for long holidays. But he did not regret the heavy workload. He thought that this was bound to happen as he took on new responsibilities and moved ahead in life.

On the job, he had always been a star performer. He was one of the few individuals in the organisation who had rapidly moved up the ladder in spite of the fact that the company attached greater importance to seniority than to merit. In 1993–94, he had won the Indira Award for Excellence given to individual employees for their commitment and contribution to the organisation. He had also got a job offer from a private company based in Kolkata. It was a lucrative job with the chance to grow faster. Even though Kolkata was his home town, he did not give the proposition a second thought. He was very content with his life and work in Mumbai.

He was disturbed when he received a fax from the corporate office in Delhi that the company had decided to transfer him to Cochin to manage the company's operations there. He was apprehensive but had no choice as the decision was taken at the highest level. The employees seldom contested such decisions. Though Ashish suspected that the transfer was due to the vested interests of a few colleagues at the Mumbai office who were jealous of him, he decided not to make it an issue; more so because the transfer came with a promotion to the post of Branch Manager and additional perks.

language barrier

Cochin is a quiet place unlike cosmopolitan Mumbai. The company provided him a car and telephone. Things were not easy for Ashish. His main problem was the language barrier. Most of the local people spoke Malayalam and it was difficult for Ashish and his family to communicate even for daily essentials like vegetables. Their only hope was the driver, Suresh, who was a local but also knew Bengali. The family felt like strangers in the land.

Ashish found the job more difficult. He had problems with the stockyard contractor, who was a local. Some of the labourers who worked under the contractor felt that they were entitled to the same privileges that were given to the permanent employees. The contractor encouraged them for his own selfish interests. Ashish could neither communicate with the contractor or the labourers directly. Though some people at the workplace tried to help him they were unable to tackle the problem. The mounting pressure affected his health.

In the meantime, he received an offer for the post of general manager of a privately managed engineering firm. The new job offered an increase in salary and a Mumbai posting. However, Ashish felt that job security would be low and he would not get much time with his family. The job would entail a lot of travel and given his poor health it was not advisable. At ISL, Ashish enjoyed the autonomy and the authority to take independent decisions. He felt that working for a private employer would curtail this freedom.

Konkona, however, opined that he should accept the offer. Life in Cochin was tough for her and the theatre scene in the city was dismal. She was worried about their son who did not have any scope for extra-curricular and self-development activities. She believed that Ashish himself needed a change and a new job would invigorate him.

After much discussion, both decided that Ashish should accept the offer. He recalled the last time he was offered a job in Mumbai and wondered how drastically the situation had changed. He was still unsure of the prudence of his decision but decided to take a chance. The day he decided to resign Ashish received a call from Delhi to inform him that he had been selected to attend a month long Advanced Marketing Training Programme at the British Industrial Society, London. This was an opportunity of a lifetime. Ashish did not want to lose this chance as he was the first and only employee to have been selected for this. After completing the training, his chances for promotion would increase. He felt that by taking up the new job at this point he would jeopardise his chances of a rewarding career at ISL. Ashish had just one day to decide. As he returned home, he thought with an uncertain heart of how to broach the subject to Konkona.

APPENDIX 5.2: COMPANY PROFILE: INDICA STEEL LTD

Indica Steel Ltd (ISL) is one of India's largest producers of steel. It is a fully integrated iron and steel maker, producing both basic and special steels for domestic construction, engineering, power, automotive and defence industries and for sale in the export market. Ranked amongst the top 20 public sector companies in the country in terms of turnover, ISL manufactures and sells a broad range of steel products, including hot and cold rolled sheets and coils, galvanised sheets, electrical sheets, structurals, plates, bars and rods, stainless steel and other alloy steels.

In 2001–2, ISL's total production of saleable steel touched a record high of 6.75 million tonnes. Of this, finished steel products contributed close to 5.25 million tonnes, semi-finished steel products 1.25 million tonnes and special alloy products 250,000 tonnes. The company's turnover in 2001–2 was Rs 111,205 million. It employed 68,000 personnel at its three integrated steel plants and offices all over India. Its plants at Kubera in Jharkhand (KSP), Rasagarh in Chhatisgarh (RSP) and at Longewaad in Maharashtra (LSP) were of international standards. The Kubera Steel Plant (KSP) had been awarded the Prime Minister's Trophy for the Best Integrated Steel Plant in India for the year 2000–1.

There is a great demand for ISL's wide range of long and flat steel products in both domestic and international markets. The main responsibility of selling these products is entrusted to ISL's own National Marketing Organisation (NMO) and Export Marketing Division. The NMO encompasses a wide network of 32 branch offices and 44 stockyards located in major cities and towns throughout the country.

NMO

The National Marketing Organisation (NMO), one of the largest marketing networks in the country, markets mild steel products from the three integrated steel plants of ISL. The NMO has its headquarters in Kolkata and the office of the director (marketing) is in New Delhi. A nationwide network of regional offices, sales offices and several strategically placed warehouses is supplemented by consignment agents and authorised dealers. A recent development in the organisation has been the reorientation of the sales branches and warehouses. This has enabled the marketing team to concentrate on building customer relationship and improving the quality of services provided. Dealer development was aggressively pursued in the rural areas to meet the customer's demand for steel in smaller quantities.

Export Marketing Division

The Export Marketing Division (EMD) of NMO manages exports of mild steel products and maintains close liaison with buyers abroad. Through the efforts of the EMD ISL steel has become a familiar and established name across the globe.

human resource development

The company believes that human resources are its greatest assets. Prime importance is attached to training and continuous development of this asset. Since the late 1950s when steel plants were being built and commissioned, ISL has striven to reach new heights in the areas of technical management and training activities, including skill development for technology upgradation, modernisation, automation and computerisation. The company's policy is dynamic and focused and stresses on moving with the changing environment. The major thrust areas for training and development include:

- Attitudinal changes.
- Optimal utilisation of existing manpower by redeployment and multi-skill training.
- Continuous training of human resources for level III and level IV automation.
- Enhancement of efficiency.
- Proper orientation/induction of new entrants.
- Safety and pollution control.
- Training in TQP.

Accordingly, training plans are prepared and are coordinated and implemented by the Management Training Institute (MTI) at Pune, the plant or unit management training centres and the corporate HRD group.

training

The various training schemes at the unit training centres of ISL include:

1. Induction programmes: Management trainees (technology and administration), junior managers (finance), operative trainees, artisan trainees and trade apprentices attend training programmes on entry into the organisation. The training period may vary from 3 months to 3 years.
2. Training of executives: Need-based general management, functional training programmes, micro-planning, action leadership training for upgradation etc. are conducted at the plant management training centres and at the MTI, Pune. The duration of these programmes vary from one to four weeks and eminent guest faculty and industry specialists conduct sessions.
3. Training of non-executives: Supervisory development functional programmes, shop floor skill development programmes, for example, unit training, refresher training schemes, redeployment training, and training in basic maintenance skills are organised at the plant or unit level.
4. Training within India: To keep abreast of developments in various specialties and functions, a number of employees, both executives and non-executives, are deputed each year to reputed training establishments, professional agencies, institutes and supplier organisations for training. Around 8–10 per cent of executives participate in such programmes every year.
5. Training abroad: For the transfer and absorption of advanced and new technologies, qualified technologists and specialists of ISL plants are deputed every year for training in countries like the USA, Russia, West Germany, the UK, Japan, Austria and Australia.

6. Manpower Development: A number of in-house programmes are conducted at the unit training institutes and the MTI. The training plans are customised to meet the needs of each plant or unit.

infrastructural facilities

The training institutes in plants and MTI, have modern infrastructural facilities like spacious classrooms, workshops and laboratories, audio-visual aids, libraries, hostels for trainees, sports and recreation facilities, playgrounds and a landscaped campus.

6

❖

challenges for future managers

Expected Learning Outcomes

♦ *Comprehend the importance of initial experiences of prospective managers in organisations.*

♦ *Analyse the mindset of prospective managers in organisational work environment and its influence in shaping managerial behaviour.*

♦ *Evaluate the impact of different approaches of prospective managers in dealing with organisational dynamics.*

Experiences in organisational dynamics during the initial 3 months are considered extremely crucial in the life of a new manager who enters the corporate sector with a set of aspirations and assumptions about his role and career growth opportunities. He steps into an organisation unaware of organisational realities and, therefore, largely unaware of what to expect and how to behave.

The experiences of both the new manager and the organisation during the initial period are important in determining the overall tone for a future relationship. The new manager creates the first personal impression in terms of his motives, attitudes, values, communication and presentation skills, personal qualities and overall behaviour. This first impression created in the minds of superiors and peers becomes relatively permanent—whether positive or negative. Similarly, the organisation also creates a first impression in the mind of a new manager. Some key experiences and events during the initial period in the life of a new entrant are considered an important aspect of learning about the individual–organisational interface—his pattern of managerial behaviour vis-à-vis other staff, the system and the culture.

FRAMEWORK FOR INTEGRATION OF FUTURE MANAGERS INTO THE ORGANISATIONAL PERSPECTIVE

After graduating in management studies an entrant is expected to assume job responsibilities as a manager in the corporate world. He is well equipped with theoretical managerial processes and skills. However, in order to execute the given role the new entrant requires firm grounding in organisational realities before he applies his knowledge and skills. This requires an integration of the classroom learning with the organisational systems. It is, therefore, important for a future manager to be concerned about the process of his integration into the organisation and then develop an organisational perspective of managing.

ENTRY INTO ORGANISATIONAL REALITIES

A prospective or future manager enters an organisation at two points:

1. As a Summer Trainee: A prospective manager joins an organisation as a summer trainee for a short internship period. During this period the trainee is largely a passive observant of organisational dynamics. Performance is more from a perspective of learning. The support and guidance of the supervisor is the main source of learning about organisational realities. Though the involvement is for a short period, yet the trainee needs to prove his worth to the organisation. The supervisor's positive approach builds in him a sense of self-confidence and a positive attitude. The organisation also provides opportunities to trainees who join it with certain expectations regarding learning outcomes. Even at this stage of limited involvement they form certain views about organisational realities. For example, when supervisors or other members of the organisation do not provide a challenging job or are not able to devote much time for mentoring or support in carrying out summer projects, trainees may form a negative opinion about the culture and people in the organisation. Summer trainees some times view organisations as ad hoc, indifferent to employees' problems, having an inefficient operational system and plagued by interpersonal conflicts affecting healthy communication across departments.

2. Job recruitment: The second entry into an organisation is at the time of final recruitment as a management trainee. At this point, the newly recruited managers become active participants of organisational realities and are subjected to positive or negative dynamics in the organisation. They are expected to be accountable for their actions from day one itself, when they are yet to develop an organisational perspective—norms, values and systems of day-to-day activities. The orientation process becomes very critical at this stage in clarifying their expectations and role in the organisation. In the absence of facilitation of reality perception, the new managers may develop misconceptions which may negatively affect their motivation, energy and performance.

ORGANISATIONAL DYNAMICS FROM MANAGERS' PERSPECTIVE

The initial experiences of managers are, therefore, critical in dealing with organisational dynamics. The likely experiences of organisational dynamics at different stages of the process of integration of new managers into organisational realities are as follows.

acceptance versus confrontation with organisational realities

1. Prospective managers use mainly two approaches at the time of joining an organisation. The first approach is largely based on theories and models taught in management schools and stereotypical views of an organisation or employer. Often, organisational realities appear in complete contrast with perceptions regarding how an organisation ought to be. Some managers adopt the confrontational approach when they find the situation inconsistent with their expectations. They become critical and may even develop a hostile attitude. They assume a rebel stance, raising their voice against apparent 'injustice' and expect a massive overhauling of the organisational system. Such an approach is perceived by other members as threatening and upsetting the normal life in the organisation. This ultimately affects their performance and their longer term survival in the organisation. These managers find it difficult to accept organisational realities and tend to resist any systemic initiative.

2. The second approach is based on the acceptance of organisational realities even if these are inconsistent with their view of the organisation. In this approach, the new managers are prepared for new experiences and open to adapt to demands of the situation. During the initial period, they make responses that are consistent with organisational requirements. An approach of acceptance helps them create their

own space in the system. In the process they develop a realistic managerial perspective.

credibility earning versus exercising organisational rights

1. This is the second stage of integration of prospective managers into the organisation. The new entrants begin to comprehend and adjust to the way the system runs. At this stage, they may further choose two sets of approaches. The first set is to earn credibility by delivering values in key result areas (KRAs). During the initial period, managers have to demonstrate self-confidence, professional knowledge, high level of energy, and skills in problem-solving, decision-making and time and work management. The credibility earned through work performance also helps them acquire organisational power—recognition and more challenging opportunities.

2. In the second approach, managers try to demand resources and support for what they are expected to accomplish. They view the organisation as weak or inadequate in handling challenges. They also harbour feelings of unfairness and injustice with respect to KRAs and in resource allocations. The demand for resources is considered a matter of right by virtue of their position or role in the organisation as opposed to the need of the situation. The performance levels of these managers are always below expectations and therefore, they generally fail to establish their credibility in the organisation.

organisational perspective on integration of new managers

The process of integration of new managers into the organisation experiences roadblocks when there is dissonance between expectations and reality both at the organisational and at the individual level.

1. Despite the criticality of the initial experiences of dynamics between an individual and an organisation, most of the time it is unplanned learning on both sides. Some individuals face disappointment on the first day of their entry into the organisation when they find the reality to be different from what they had imagined. Others are pleasantly surprised and feel proud to be part of the organisation. Similarly, the organisation may regret or be happy to have recruited certain employees. While recruiting new staff may be routine for the organisation, for the new entrant it is crucial as it lays the foundation of a productive future. Some organisations follow a well-defined process for the entry of a new manager, while others are extremely casual.

2. However, hardly any organisation holds itself accountable for the negative behaviour of a manager. The negative events in the organisation are generally attributed to individual factors. When such incidents occur frequently in the organisation, it may be concluded that either the recruitment policy and method is faulty, or the organisational systems or culture is not conducive to creating a positive impact on a new manager. Organisations do pay a big price for neglecting the process of grooming an employee during his initial period of joining the organisation. Most organisations cope with problems caused by a new manager by transferring him from one job to another, until they ask him to leave.

3. New managers have certain images of the workplace which are largely based on social stereotypes such as an independent, well furnished office, well equipped with high quality computers, clearly defined job roles, a supportive culture and systematic procedures. Social background, educational practices and cultural upbringing contribute to such stereotypes. These have implications for the way the organisation

influences the behaviour of a new manager. Some of the initial experiences become instrumental in the shaping or learning of managerial behaviour. A planned approach to socialising new managers contributes towards developing a more realistic perspective of the organisation.

CASES ON CHALLENGES FOR FUTURE MANAGERS

Six cases have been included in this module that explore the relevance of integration process of a prospective manager in the overall development of managerial behaviour. Of these, four are related to summer trainees and two describe new managers who were recently recruited. The cases highlight issues pertaining to prospective managers while they struggle between being learners and performers or are in the process of integrating their individual personality with the organisational perspective.

Two cases on summer trainees describe the initial jolts they received when they became aware of the prevalent discrepancies in the stipend. 'Training—A Two-Way Process' describes a person who, after having observed this discrepancy in her stipend, took up the challenge to prove her worth to the organisation. Subsequently, the top management acknowledged her contribution in winning a sales pitch.

In 'Realisation of a Dream', the trainee's stipend was reduced after he had joined. He took this in his stride and adopted an innovative approach to establish his credibility. He finally succeeded in his intentions and the organisation paid him a bonus at the end of his training. These cases illustrate approaches based on acceptance and credibility earning.

Contrary to these, in 'The Art of Dealing with Management', a summer trainee became a victim of her own perception of what the organisation should be. Her experience led her to perceive most aspects of the organisation as chaotic, disorderly and messy and consequently her level of satisfaction dropped. This case illustrates an attitude of confrontation with organisational realities.

A similar experience is narrated in 'Compromises'. The trainee had problems in completing his project work due to lack of adequate facilities. Instead of complaining, he worked out an alternate route to complete his work.

The next two cases describe new recruits in the organisation. In 'A Balanced View' the recruit had an excellent track record of achievements in sports. He represented the company successfully in several sports tournaments. However, at the time of promotion, another colleague was promoted ahead of him, though both worked in the same position. The case demonstrates how a manager can lack an understanding of the organisational perspective.

In 'Ego Clashes' the candidate had joined the organisation with set expectations. He was soon stressed out by the organisational work culture which was quite different from his view of how the organisation should be. His social and educational background made it difficult for him to accept the reality. He used the confrontational approach in dealing with the organisational processes and systems.

REFERENCES

Becker, E. Brian, Huselid, Mark A. and Ulrich, Dave. (2001). *The HR scorecard: Linking people, strategy, and performance.* Boston, MA: Harvard Business School Press.

Butcher, David and Clarke, Martin. (2002). Organisational politics: The cornerstone for organisational democracy. *Organisational Dynamics, 31*(1), 35–46.

Furnham, A. (2000). Work in 2020: Prognostications about the world of work twenty years into the millennium. *Journal of Management Psychology, 15*(3), 242–254.

Habbel, Rolf W. (2002, first quarter). The human(e) factor: Nurturing a leadership culture. *Strategy+Business*. www.strategy-business.com.

Hill, Ronald Paul and Stephens, Debra Lynn. (2003). The compassionate organisation in the 21st century. *Organisational Dynamics*, *32*(4), 331–341.

Kast, Fremont E. and Rosenzweig, James. (1985). *Organisation and management, fourth edition*. New York: McGraw-Hill.

Khandwalla, Pradip N. (1977). *The design of organisations*. New York: Harcourt Brace Jovanovich, Inc.

Mike, Barry and Slocum Jr, John W. (2003). Slice of reality: Changing culture at Pizza Hut and Yum! Brands, Inc. *Organisational Dynamics*, *32*(4), 319–330.

CASES ON CHALLENGES FOR FUTURE MANAGERS

key learnings

♦ *Analyse the effects of discrimination on management trainees based on their institutional affiliation.*

♦ *Explore the dynamics of new managers in dealing with disillusionment resulting from a mismatch between expectations and reality.*

♦ *Appreciate the value of initiative in building credibility.*

♦ *Evaluate the first impression of summer internees in shaping their managerial behaviours.*

TRAINING—A TWO-WAY PROCESS*

Anubhuti was elated, she had been selected as a summer intern by Sunrise Company. She had just completed the first year of the postgraduation programme at the Indian School of Management, Ahmedabad (ISMA). Though she was a sincere student, she felt that her marks did not adequately reflect her competency. She had applied to several companies that had visited the campus but was eliminated in the interview rounds. She attributed this not to her underperformance but to the company's selection procedure. Her area of interest was marketing and she did not want to compromise by taking up any other offer. Her desire to work in this field with a reputed company was fulfilled when Sunrise selected her.

first experience

Sunrise was a well-known company with several strategic business units. She had been assigned to the International Business Development (IBD) unit. She was happy as the profile offered was of sales and marketing. She wanted to do a good project and give her best to it. Sunrise had offered her a consolidated stipend of Rs 7,000. Excited at the thought of the orientation programme and the other interns she would get to work with, Anubhuti arrived at the office in Mumbai.

While she waiting for the programme to begin, she talked to some of the other interns. One was from IFT and another from Premier Institute, Indore. She learned that both of them had been offered a stipend of Rs 10,000. Anubhuti was struck. Why had Sunrise offered them a higher stipend? Why this discrimination? Feeling let down, she wanted to leave. But as she had really wanted to work here, she decided to stay on and raise the issue when the time was right.

*Acknowledgements: Harnoor Channi, Kanika Mittal, Rohan Tiwary and Sanjay Sharma.

project allocation

Mr Kelkar, a senior manager in the Customer Relationship Management (CRM) department, introduced them to the allocated projects. The task was to test the feasibility of certain programmes that the IDB unit wanted to implement in the near future. Their research and subsequent report would form the basis for the implementation. Anubhuti was given the project of designing entry strategies for the aqua product that IBD wanted to launch. She had read about it in the newspapers and was happy as she believed that it was best of all the projects.

Shaken by the disparity in the stipend, she approached Mr Kelkar after the meeting. He was dismissive of the issue. Choosing to be non-committal, he said that it was a policy decision taken by the HR department. He advised Anubhuti to concentrate more on the work at hand. Anubhuti was dismayed. She had excitedly looked forward to the first day and this confrontation left her disenchanted and angry. She was disheartened because she thought that she was as capable as the other interns and felt that they had been offered a higher stipend since they were from more reputed institutes. She was informed that she had to leave the next day for her first work station, Secunderabad. She thought whether she had made the right choice of company.

the right choice

The department Anubhuti joined had one manager and 18 traders. She had to conduct research on the transportation facility and market feasibility for the product. She started out dispiritedly. Over the next 2 months all her interactions with the manager and traders was via email. However, she was determined not to let this affect her performance and she did her best. The manager and traders were helpful which motivated her. As she had to work alone, at times she felt cut off from the other departments and was unaware of how they worked. But she continued to work sincerely.

As the training period drew to a close, Anubhuti looked back at the past 2 months. The formal atmosphere she had initially expected was not there. Her department workers were good and hard working, but were not stiff and formal. The manager was genuinely concerned about her welfare, and did not pester her to do her job. She had been provided with a comfortable accommodation. Due to the heavy workload she could not remain in contact with the other interns, but she had learned a lot and enjoyed herself. Her past disillusions faded away.

success

Anubhuti returned to the head office and began to prepare her report. She was keen to make a strong, positive impact by the thoroughness of her report. At office she was relaxed and interacted freely with her colleagues. As the day for the final presentation drew near, she was full of nervous energy.

Her presentation was the first. The presence of the CEO and all department heads made her simultaneously happy and nervous. She made a confident presentation of the figures and inferences she had drawn on the basis of the field studies. It was well received. After all the presentations were over, she was called and informed that the board had decided to launch the product on the basis of her report and recommendation!

REALISATION OF A DREAM*

Nearing the end of his first year of postgraduation at the Gujarat Management Institute (GMI), Rohan was confident of his performance which had been very good throughout and his professors and classmates appreciated his sincerity. Everyone expected him to get a good offer for his summer internship. Rohan was clear about the sector and the kind of company in which he wanted to work.

*Acknowledgements: Harnoor Channi, Kanika Mittal, Rohan Tiwary and Sanjay Sharma.

He had always been interested in a career in advertising. His choice of companies included JWT, O&M and Aakriti Advertising. Advertising agencies generally visited campuses towards the end of the placement activities and were considered second choices. He was clear about what he wanted and was confident of his abilities to achieve it. The process of selection went smoothly and he was one of the two students who were selected by Aakriti. For Rohan, it was the beginning of his journey for building a career. He was posted in Mumbai, he had heard a lot about the city and the opportunities it offered for growth and learning. He looked forward to the experience. Rohan reached Mumbai two days before the joining date so that he could arrange for an accommodation. The stipend of Rs 3,500 was too little to manage. However, he did not complain because he looked at the internship period not as an opportunity to earn, but to learn as much as possible.

Rohan got up earlier than usual, he was aware of the traffic snarls in Mumbai and did not want to report late on the first day of work. He set out from the guest house where he was staying with a lot of expectations and determination to make his mark at work. Reaching the office of Aakriti, he liked what he saw. The building was impressive and the infrastructure excellent. The HR manager met him and apprised him of the work culture and environment. She also briefed him about his job requirements and responsibilities. He was introduced to the other staff members and to Mr Ramnik, one of the general managers of the agency.

Rohan had his own cubicle and computer. On the first day itself his immediate superior, Rajesh, allotted substantial work to him. Rohan was impressed by the professional and competitive environment. The organisation had a relatively flat structure and employees were encouraged to express their views openly. There was no rigid power structure.

The first day went off well till Rohan received a call from the HR manager who wanted to meet him. She informed him that his stipend had been reduced to Rs 2,500. He was surprised and when he questioned her, she informed him that it was a policy decision of the agency not to pay more than this figure to summer interns. Realising the futility of the situation, Rohan did not

argue. The HR manager assured him that the policy was likely
to be revised soon. Rohan had mixed feelings about his first day
at work. On the one hand, he liked the people and the working
environment; on the other hand, he was unhappy with the manner
in which the agency had gone back on its word.

The next day Rohan was assigned to his pilot project—preparing a communication strategy for the soon-to-be launched retail
outlets of Reliance Petroleum. He was free to approach anyone
in the office for any assistance that he required. Mr Ramnik told
him that it was an important project and if he prepared a feasible
report of recommendation, his suggestions would be incorporated
in the final presentation made to Reliance Petroleum. However,
he advised Rohan to approach him only in the case of extremely
important matters as he had a busy schedule. Mr Ramnik was
one of seven general managers in the agency but he handled major
accounts, worth Rs 550 crore (Rs 5.5 billion) of Aakriti's total
billing of Rs 700 crore (Rs 7 billion). He encouraged Rohan to
come up with innovative ideas and a concrete outline. After this
conversation Rohan felt motivated. It obliterated all memories
of the previous day's bad experience. He sensed a big opportunity
to learn and grow and wanted to give it his best shot.

The next day he chalked out a plan of action for the project.
He planned a survey of all the petrol pumps in Mumbai and the
neighbouring areas to study consumer behaviour and buying
habits. He was required to report to the office in the morning
and at the end of each day's work. At times he was frustrated
when the sites were close to his guest house, but he had to commute across the city to report at the office. He discussed this
issue with Mahesh, who told him that he could report later if the
site was far off from the office.

During these field trips Rohan interacted with many people
from different strata of society, from rich petrol pump owners to
poor truck drivers and their helpers. This exposure gave him insight into consumer demographics. The truck drivers played the
most important role in the choice of lubricants and the petrol
pumps from where they bought them. Understanding the psychographics of this segment would help Rohan develop an effective

communication strategy to position the concept. He decided to spend some time with the truck drivers in their own environment to better understand their preferences and attitudes.

He discussed this with Mahesh, but he was not very enthusiastic about this idea. Some of the other people he talked to also dissuaded him. Nevertheless Rohan was convinced that the exercise would provide valuable information and help make their strategy more effective. He approached Mr Ramnik who was impressed with Rohan's idea and commended him for taking the initiative. Mr Ramnik provided him a hand-held camera and a voice recorder to tape all his interactions.

Rohan travelled by truck on an eight-day journey from Mumbai to Ambala. The truck driver was Sardar Joginder Singh Lakkha. He recorded 76 hours of conversation and 22 hours of video. This exercise yielded valuable data on the psychographics of the end-users of Reliance Petroleum. All this would not have been possible without the encouragement and support of Mr Ramnik.

After returning from Ambala he began work on his report. He was confident that his strategy would justify the faith the company had reposed in him. His final report was appreciated by everyone who read it. Mr Ramnik promised to incorporate the recommendations in the final report to be presented to the client. The next day Mr Ramnik summoned him to his office and asked him to make the final presentation before the client! Rohan was happy that his hard work had paid off. Five of his seven suggestions were incorporated.

He put up a good show and his suggestions were well received by the client. At the end of the presentation Mr Ramnik made a special mention of Rohan's involvement in the project and his sincerity. It was the end of his assignment and summer internship. He was happy with the way things turned out, his involvement in the successful pitching of another major account by Aakriti. On the last day of office he was felicitated at a gathering by Mr Ramnik who presented him a cheque of Rs 10,000 as bonus in recognition of his efforts and the profit he had brought to the company.

176 of Shaping Organisational Strategies

THE ART OF DEALING WITH MANAGEMENT*

The news seemed too good to be true. Sheetal had been selected for summer internship by Acme Advertising Limited after a 5-minute interview! The panel had merely asked her about her hometown and familiarity with Delhi. Though the reputation of her institute, ANC Institute of Management, drew major companies for campus recruitment, being selected by the fifth largest advertising agency in the country was no small feat. She had always been confused between account planning and brand management as a career and the summer programme would help her decide. Her institute made arrangements for her stay on the IIT campus, which was not far from Acme's office. She had been offered a paltry stipend of Rs 3,000, but this did not bother her as she was more concerned about learning from her experience at the agency.

However, she was in for a shock when she arrived at the office the next day: the HR department was not aware that she was coming and no arrangements had been made for her. After a while the Director came to welcome her and showed her around the office. Probably because she was from a premier institute, she was even taken out for lunch. Later, her project guide explained to her the nature of her duties and she felt better.

The next day she went to office expecting organised work and further orientation. To her astonishment, there was no further communication from her superiors. As the day drew to a close, Sheetal realised that she was on her own. She had to make the best of her situation and manage by herself. Having an analytical bent of mind she observed the functioning of the organisation. Though small, it had a complex hierarchy. There was no constant pressure and the atmosphere was casual. No power distance was maintained between juniors and seniors and the Director himself dropped by several times to talk to her. An average day in the

*Acknowledgements: Harnoor Channi, Kanika Mittal, Rohan Tiwary and Sanjay Sharma.

organisation began post-lunch. Before lunch most of the client servicing people were out in the field. When they returned with work or orders after lunch, the account planners got down to work. Though one had to report to office by 10 a.m., work started only around 1 p.m. and continued up to 8 p.m.

Her profile was that of a junior account planner. Her projects portfolio included several major industry players. She enjoyed the hands-on learning experience. Though her project guide was a busy person, he offered her help and guidance whenever required. She was given differential treatment in many ways. While other trainees were engaged in research, she got a chance to work on live projects. They looked up to her as at a higher position. This sense of importance led to mixed feelings in Sheetal. She did not know if this was due to her work or on account of her being from a premier institute. Her ideas were listened to and appreciated, though rarely implemented. After a few days she was not sure if she was having a good summer or a bad one. She began to feel disillusioned.

The environment at the office was chaotic. People were always looking for free time when the boss was not around or talking about better paid jobs in other agencies. Most of them viewed this as a transitional job to make some money and then move on. Sheetal could not understand why an organisation with such resources and fame could not retain its employees and create a more professional and competitive work atmosphere. The level of passion and commitment was low. There was no reward or incentive apart from an occasional celebration party when a major account was secured. The efficiency of an employee was measured in terms of the hours put in and not in terms of the quality of work. Participation in decision-making was poor, so was dissemination of information. For example, an employee whose wife was pregnant called to ask if the medical expenses would be reimbursed by the agency and realised that the company had changed its medicare reimbursement policy without informing any one. For a meeting scheduled at 9 a.m. people would start to trickle in at 11:30 a.m. and the meeting would begin around the afternoon. Attendance was usually low unless the employees were specifically directed to be present. This lack of passion demotivated Sheetal. Though her own projects were good, she did not feel happy at the end of the day. Her perception of summer internship as a means to learn, set goals and achieve them and understand how organisations work was proved wrong at every step.

Sheetal worked 10–12 hours every day, including Sundays. She never asked for a holiday as she wanted to make the most of her internship. The pressure of work varied from very high to very low and she disliked dealing with these swings as they made her uncomfortable. However, there were many informal opportunities to discuss decisions. Several times she got to work on some excellent assignments. Perhaps, her boss could perceive the relative inefficiency of the other employees and allotted the work to Sheetal.

When her internship came to an end she did not know what to write in her report. Her work had been good, her research and presentations were well received. However, despite repeated requests the HR department did not issue her an official letter of appraisal. Sheetal returned to her institute without a formal appraisal letter or many good memories. She could always go to the office again to have the appraisal form filled. What bothered her was if, after the experience, she would be able to motivate herself enough to work in an advertising agency again.

COMPROMISES*

A clear vision of a career in marketing inspired Aryan to enrol for the PG diploma course in business management offered by the Premier Institute, Indore, in 2002. Besides his first year of theoretical knowledge, he had great expectations from his summer training.

*Acknowledgements: Harnoor Channi, Kanika Mittal, Rohan Tiwary and Sanjay Sharma.

challenging projects

At the end of the first year of his course, Aryan was ready to test the theories he had learned by working on live projects. Since he wanted to work on a brand management project during his summer internship, he applied to BT Advertising Limited when they came for campus recruitment. He prepared thoroughly for the recruitment process and was the only student from the institute who made it through the rigorous group discussion and personal interview rounds. He had expressed a desire during the interview to work on a project on brand management and the panel had agreed to consider his request. Aryan felt contented.

He walked confidently into the office on his first day. Being from a premier institute, he expected a certain amount of respect. To his surprise, he was allotted an obsolete computer and a broken chair in a backroom and given an old information booklet to familiarise himself with the organisation. For the rest of the period of internship he used his own laptop. Towards the end of the day his superior, much older than him, called him and Aryan thought that he would be assigned some concrete work; but he only made small talk.

This was a preview of the rest of his internship. He was assigned two projects—retailer push and visibility audit, and an assessment of BT's image in the market. This was a far cry from the project on brand management that he had been promised. Feeling cheated, Aryan discussed this with his superior. In his typical laidback manner, he informed Aryan that these were the only projects available at the moment. Aryan was disillusioned as he realised that he would be spending all his time doing market research.

The office culture was a far cry from what he had expected. There were no fixed working hours. He was not required to be present in the office all the time. He could work from home and go to office only to submit reports or attend a meeting. Aryan found his forte in the weekly meetings of the marketing division. His suggestions were innovative and were taken seriously by others. This motivated him to strategise better. There was not much power distance across the hierarchies. The relaxed environment did not put any pressure on him.

At the end of 2 months, Aryan submitted his reports. His boss was appreciative of his efforts and remarked that he would make a good manager. Aryan walked out of the office that evening with a smile on his face but discontentment in his heart. There was a sense of futility in the work he had done. His expectations had remained unfulfilled.

A BALANCED VIEW*

It was well past midnight, Sumit Verma was studying for the Blaze Airlines executive officer written examination. After studying all night, he left for the examination at 9 a.m. He did well and within a week he received an interview call letter. The interview was to be held in Delhi.

Sumit reached the corporate office of Blaze Airlines half an hour early. He met Mr Gupta, the MD of Delhi division, who was impressed by Sumit's excellence in sports, particularly his participation in football matches at the state level. When he asked Sumit how he maintained a balance between studies and sports, Sumit replied that it was the result of good time management. He was confident of his performance and as expected, he received confirmation of his selection, asking him to join the Delhi office within a week.

The first day Sumit reached the office 15 minutes early. He was happy to learn that his immediate boss was Mr Gupta. When Mr Gupta arrived in the office, he called Sumit into his cabin and welcomed him to the new job. He also told him to play football matches for Blaze Airlines, an offer which Sumit gladly accepted. He was pleased with the welcome he had received.

*Acknowledgements: Ajay Nayar, Amit Tripathi, Sanjukta Ghosh and Vivek Saraswat.

practice sessions

From day one sumit put in all his efforts in his work. Two weeks later Mr Gupta informed him that he had to go to Cochin the following week to play a match against Indian Railways. Since the dates of the match clashed with an important meeting, Sumit was told not to worry and practice for the match. Mr Gupta assigned his work to Sumit's colleague, Atul. Every morning Sumit went for practice sessions and reached the office an hour or two late. Feeling a time crunch, he tried to strike a balance between his work and football practice.

Sumit's team lost the match and he attributed the defeat to his lack of sufficient practice. On returning to Delhi he told Mr Gupta to inform him in advance before the next match so that he had enough time to practice. Mr Gupta agreed and Sumit was happy that his superior was encouraging him.

However, some of his colleagues did not like his proximity to Mr Gupta and the concessions at work he was receiving. Atul was particularly antagonistic and would often discuss the issue with others. Things continued like this for a while, Sumit was aware of the situation but did not take it seriously. Some people would ask him in a mocking tone, 'How is your practice going on, Sumit?' or 'You have become very busy now, you don't have any time for us.' Due to the limited time he spent in the office he did not develop friendly relations with his colleagues.

The second match was organised after 3 months. By then he was practising seriously and was determined to win. Since the match was held in Delhi, his colleagues and Mr Gupta went to see it. He performed well and scored a goal, and his team won the match. The next day when he reached the office many people congratulated him. Elated with his good performance, he devoted more energy to football practice.

It was 6 months since Sumit had joined Blaze Airlines and it was time for the half-yearly performance appraisal of the office staff. On the basis of this appraisal, trainees were selected for promotion. Sumit was confident of being promoted. However, the report revealed that Atul had been promoted. Sumit had received a positive appraisal for his extra-curricular activities but Atul, who did extra work in his absence, was considered a better candidate for promotion.

monetary incentive

Sumit felt dejected. He felt he was being penalised for having participated in the tournament, even if for the company. He met Mr Gupta the next day and voiced his feelings. Mr Gupta told him that Atul had performed well and had completed Sumit's assignments in his absence. At the same time he promised to talk to the management to reconsider its decision of not promoting Sumit and also to recommend a monetary incentive for his excellent performance that earned laurels for the company.

EGO CLASHES*

After graduating in computer engineering, Sanjay and some of his friends were selected by Bitech, a leading software company, during campus recruitment. Born and brought up in Bengal, it was the first time he was going far away from home and that, too, to a fast-paced city like Mumbai. They joined the company with high expectations but were shocked by the work culture. Sanjay was inducted into a 3-month training programme. The daily schedule involved at least 12 hours of work in addition to 3 hours of commuting. Sanjay and his friends resented the pressure. Having communist leanings, they felt that software programmers were a highly exploited lot.

*Acknowledgements: Ajay Nayar, Amit Tripathi, Sanjukta Ghosh and Vivek Saraswat.

at a disadvantage

Sanjay was inducted into a project even before his training was over. The other five members of the team were, all experienced. He was at a disadvantage as he was not familiar with the core area. The project leader (PL), Mr Gupta, had 10 years of work experience. He had joined Bitech a year ago and this was the second project he was heading. He expected Sanjay to pick up the required skills on the job. The project began on the same day when Sanjay and his friends had planned to go home. Seeing his friends leave for home incensed Sanjay. The initial phase was difficult for him as he struggled to learn and meet his deadlines. Further, a few incidents created a rift between him and his PL.

'irresponsibility'

One day Sanjay finished his work early and left at 6p.m. The next day Mr Gupta called him and rebuked him, 'Who asked you to go home yesterday? I had work for you in the night. Things here do not work as you think. You have to abide by the rules.' Sanjay apologised and promised to inform him in future before leaving. Sanjay thought that his boss was being vindictive by keeping his employees till 9 p.m. On another occasion, Sanjay took leave as he was running fever. When he reached the office the next day, Mr Gupta was infuriated and called him a highly irresponsible person. A delivery had to be made to the client the previous day and Sanjay was supposed to have worked on it. In his absence Mr Gupta had to do the work himself.

The third major incident took place when some delivery had to be made. Mr Gupta asked him to complete the assigned work and submit it within 3 hours. Getting down to work, Sanjay realised that it was more difficult than he had anticipated. He committed an error in coding and the work stretched on till evening. He was scared to report the matter to Mr Gupta and tried to rectify the error himself. Concerned by the delay Mr Gupta decided to check for himself. When he found the work incomplete he lost his cool and gave Sanjay a piece of his mind. Finally, he asked one of the more experienced employees to complete the job.

That day Sanjay returned home completely disillusioned. He was no longer enthusiastic about his work. There were problems in his personal life as well; he could not adjust to the food and found commuting time consuming. Not being fluent in Hindi, communication became a problem. The fast pace of life put him off.

conflicts

From then on Sanjay and Mr Gupta rarely spoke to each other. Sanjay did not like the PL and did not discuss his problems with him. On his part Mr Gupta thought Sanjay had a negative attitude towards work and lost no opportunity to point out his mistakes. Once Mr Gupta picked on him publicly during a meeting and accused him of taking too much leave. The fact was that Sanjay had taken only two days' leave. This resulted in a heated argument. Once Sanjay spent the entire weekend working to meet a deadline, but Mr Gupta did not acknowledge his work. Attending office became a torture for Sanjay.

The final day of the project dawned. Sanjay had been working under tremendous pressure to avoid any adverse remark from Mr Gupta. Finally the project was over and Sanjay was relieved. He was mentally exhausted; his dream of the 'great IT opportunity' had been shattered. The next month no project was assigned to him and he spent time familiarising himself with the environment and work culture at Bitech.

The next month he was assigned to a new project. When he came to know that the PL was Mr Gupta, he was very upset. He wondered why Mr Gupta had selected him again. His appraisal was also due. Sanjay spent the entire day wondering what to do. The next day he applied for leave to go home. He did not wait for Mr Gupta to ask him why he wanted to go. He packed his bags and left, never to return to the office.

7

❖

mentoring and empowerment

Expected Learning Outcomes

♦ *Identify the role of mentoring and empowerment in the context of the global business scenario.*

♦ *Analyse issues and problems that managers experience in the face of inadequate arrangements for empowerment and mentoring.*

♦ *Comprehend the process of instituting effective empowerment and mentoring processes.*

Across industry segments, centralised and long-term corporate strategies and planning are proving inadequate to meet the challenges of a diversified and heterogeneous consumer segment. There is a shift from the 'one size fits all' (Hamilton and Scandura, 2003). Earlier, a centralised corporate strategy was considered sufficient and suitable for the entire organisation. However, discontinuous and complex changes in the market and in technologies are bringing about diversification and segmentation in the typical consumer profile (Hill and Stephens, 2003). Simultaneously, as organisations spread their reach across the world, the need to understand the diversity within the workforce and the necessity to cater to individual needs also makes a centralised policy cumbersome and inhibiting (Huselid, Becker and Ulrich, 2001).

Organisations are waking up to this fact and adopting practices that help them adapt to market-oriented organisational processes in which managers participate in the decision-making process at their level of functioning. Organisations are increasingly realising that they can no longer draw upon the company's strategies and policies that can guide a manager in taking decisions in the local territory of business operations. To be able to handle this enhanced freedom and responsibility, organisations are providing their employees with mentoring programmes that are customised to individual requirements and job profiles (Hamilton and Scandura, 2003; James, 2003).

MENTORING AND EMPOWERMENT IN THE CURRENT ORGANISATIONAL CONTEXT

Mentoring is an organisational programme that helps managers develop capabilities to meet organisational challenges concerning their work responsibilities. Mentorship provides an opportunity to a new member of an organisation to learn from another manager who is more experienced (Hill and Stephens, 2003). Empowerment, on the other hand, is an organisational process for delegating autonomy to lower management people with enhanced capacities to take their decisions or actions that are in the best interest of the organisation (Huselid, Becker and Ulrich, 2001). Both mentoring and empowerment help in creating an environment of achievement and productivity as managers require personalised guidance and support. This equips them to accept independent responsibility for tasks within their work sphere, take decisions in the face of uncertainty and function as change agents in the best interest of the organisation rather than mere adaptors to change. Mentoring and empowerment are mutually dependent. Organisations that lag in instituting the processes of empowerment and mentoring may experience difficulties in the efficient delivery of products and services both to their internal and external clients (Johnson and Macy, 2001). Managers become extremely frustrated when they find themselves in situations where they have the competence to take decisions but are organisationally bound to wait for orders from the top management. Similarly, in the absence of effective mentoring processes, managers cannot be equipped to use organisational autonomy for taking independent decisions.

dynamics of mentoring

Mentoring is an organisational intervention to ensure that new managers are integrated into the organisational framework of empowerment. Also, employees in various stages of their career look for enhancement of skills and competencies through this process. Honing of professional skills equips them to handle organisational dynamics in a proactive and efficient manner. A well-intended empowerment policy will not be effective unless the managers are competent to handle the independence. Mentoring brings about this competency level and confidence and paves the way for personal professional, and organisational growth.

The first step towards mentoring is need assessment. A realistic assessment of the individual's current competencies, required skills and training areas is important for developing a customised mentoring programme. Unlike internship, mentoring is a continuous process. New recruits undergo a period of internship where they are oriented into the organisation and its systems (Habbel, 2002). This may last from a few days to a few months. At the end of this phase, recruits are expected to assume full managerial responsibilities. In mentoring, it is understood that employees need continuous upgradation of skills and competencies. The mentor offers a supportive role to the protégé. The protégé may take the mentor's help to test ideas, develop proficiencies, bring in attitudinal modifications and chart a productive career path. The selection of a suitable mentor is a sensitive exercise. Globalisation has brought in its wake increased diversity in the work environment and culture. Social culture, gender, language, educational background and prior work experience have to be taken into account while assigning a mentor to an employee (Matson, Patiath and Shavers, 2003). The interpersonal dynamics play a significant role not only in the success of the mentor–protégé relationship, but also in the effectiveness of the association in bringing about positive changes in the employee's productivity. There has to be a certain degree of compatibility in the pairing for an authentic exchange of ideas. The parties concerned may also make mid-term reviews to assess the success of the association. The mentor is ideally a person who is able to gauge objectively the protégé's proficiency and competency level without encroaching on his work sphere. At times more than one mentor is engaged for the same person. Each one addresses a different need area and may work with other mentors as a team to develop a comprehensive mentorship programme for the individual.

The internal culture influences the kind of mentor available for employees (Hill and Stephens, 2003). Some organisations may allocate mentors on the basis of seniority, others on grounds of functional expertise. A large organisation with a hierarchical structure may prefer a mentorship programme based on seniority and experience. More open organisations may experiment with area expertise in allotting mentors to employees. Thus, a person may be younger in age and experience in the company, but may act as mentor to a more senior member who wants to upgrade his skills.

'Team mentoring' is another concept that has gained popularity. Instead of a one–one relationship, in team mentorship one person acts as the mentor to a group of employees. There are team activities and discussions, along with individual sessions with each member, where each person's proficiencies are mapped to identify the areas which require greater focus. Working in a team in a mentorship programme has the advantage of the team acting as a support group for each member.

dynamics of empowerment

Empowerment is a developmental and systemic process in an organisational environment. As a development process it helps the employee become aware of his potential, identify opportunities and possible resistance in the work environment, and enhance his current competence to become self-reliant. As a systemic process, empowerment creates systems and structures that enable the employee to take initiative, make decisions, and within the scope of the work environment, assume responsibility and accountability for work accomplished.

Developmental and systemic processes need to be established through practice, precept and experience. An assessment procedure that identifies the potential and talent of employees, and provides training and counselling facilities for enhancing capability to take decisions and act independently contributes towards empowerment. Changes in attitude, values systems and style of management create an environment of trust and achievement.

A typical hierarchical, bureaucratic structure is not conducive for empowering employees in the work environment. Lengthy channels of authority and decision-making slow down the process of decision-making and efficient implementation of policies. Decentralisation has been observed to have a positive impact on the process of empowerment and delegation of authority. A flat organisational structure, performance-driven incentive systems, autonomous entrepreneurial centres (SBUs—Strategic Business Units), developing authority relationships based on competence and performance, and internal marketing orientations are some of the processes organisations have successfully adopted towards empowering staff at various levels (Halal, 1994). Matrix structures encourage cross-referencing and multi-tasking and generates an environment of mutual sharing of resources and encourages resourcefulness. An empowered employee finds ample scope to demonstrate skills of independent enquiry and implementation. Delegation is an important component of empowerment. Task delegation is the first step towards attributing greater potential to the employee and encouraging enhanced performance.

As an organisational process, empowerment entails replacing a system of overprotectiveness, patriarchal attitudes and authoritarian model with an environment of exploration and risk-taking, independent decision-making, assuming responsibility for decisions taken and a democratic work pattern. Empowerment is to be preceded by having in place a programme of orientation and training both for the subordinate and the superior. From the subordinate's perspective, empowerment means increased responsibility, more functional independence, accountability for one's actions, risk-taking and enhanced scope for personal and career growth. The superior may initially feel threatened by the apparent loss of power, reduced control and possible loss of authority. On the positive side, there is freeing up of work time to focus attention on tasks more relevant at a higher organisational level. The manager transforms from a mere follower of orders to an active contributor to organisational growth. There is shared responsibility instead of trickling down of orders.

CASES ON MENTORING AND EMPOWERMENT

This module includes four cases, two on the systemic aspects of empowerment, and two on the developmental processes of empowerment and mentoring. The first two cases highlight the consequences of lack of organisational orientation toward empowerment and mentoring. 'From Darkness to Light' and 'Turning the Tide' describe two women from rural areas who were transformed through empowerment and mentoring processes despite social constraints. These women in turn motivated other poor women and also gained international exposure. Though these two cases are not from the corporate sector, they are discussed here to illustrate the process of transformation as integral with empowerment. Many corporate sector companies are moving to gain market share in rural and semi-urban areas and need to create support programmes in local areas with the local people. The processes of transformation presented in these two cases add tremendous value to business corporations.

'Nurturing Talent' describes a person with knowledge and expertise who enjoyed high credibility among his team members. However, his individualistic way of handling work made his colleagues overdependent on him. He was shocked when his superior rated him low on team-building skills. The case illustrates mentoring and empowerment as important skills in the process of team-building.

'Winning Ways' focuses on a person who possessed leadership skills and was good at team building. The organisation that he joined, however, lacked both developmental and systemic processes of empowerment. With his capabilities being underutilised, he soon found himself at the crossroads where he did not know where to go and what to do in the organisation. There was relief when a like-minded person joined the department and offered to help him. He regained his confidence but, in the light of past events, decided to quit the organisation.

REFERENCES

Habbel, Rolf W. (2002, first quarter). The human(e) factor: Nurturing a leadership culture. *Strategy+Business*. www.strategy-business.com.

Halal, William E. (1994). From hierarchy to enterprise: Internal markets are the new foundation of management. *Academy of Management Executive*, *8*(4), 69–83.

Hamilton, Betti A. and Scandura, Terri A. (2003). E-mentoring: Implications for organisational learning and development in a wired world. *Organisational Dynamics*, *31*(4), 388–402.

Hill, Ronald Paul and Stephens, Debra Lynn. (2003). The compassionate organisation in the 21st century. *Organisational Dynamics, 32*(4), 331–341.

Huselid, Mark A., Becker, Brian E. and Ulrich, David. (2001). *Linking people, strategy, and performance.* Boston, MA: Harvard Business School Press.

James, Constance R. (2003). Designing learning organisations. *Organisational Dynamics, 32*(1), 46–61.

Johnson, Douglas B. and Macy, Granger. (2001). Using environmental paradigms to understand and change an organisation's response to stakeholders. *Journal of Organisational Change Management, 14*(4), 314–334.

Matson, Eric, Patiath, Pradip and Shavers, Tim. (2003). Stimulating knowledge sharing: Strengthening your organisation's internal knowledge market. *Organisational Dynamics, 32*(3), 275–285.

CASES ON MENTORING AND EMPOWERMENT

key learnings

♦ *Identify the role of empowerment in achieving organisational objective.*

♦ *Assess the hierarchical organisational set-up as a major source of conflict and overlapping.*

♦ *Experience how development initiative empowers women at the grass roots level through a process of transformation.*

FROM DARKNESS TO LIGHT*

Gauri belonged to an Iyer Brahmin family of Kutch, Gujarat. Her birth went unsung in the gloom of having had a girl child. She was merely considered a burden on the family. The patriarchal society defined her limits within the four walls of her house. The family owned 2 acres of land that was insufficient to provide even two square meals a day. Frequent droughts made the land highly unproductive. Considering that even her brother was not sent to school, education for Gauri was an impossible dream.

years of struggle

As she grew up, an increasing amount of familial responsibility was thrust on her. Hardly into her teens, she began to work in the cotton fields for 12 hours a day, for a meager daily wage of Rs 5. She had to walk 8 km every day to fetch drinking water. Despite all these hardships, she was happy to be able to do something for her family. Gauri did not have any personal dreams for herself. She only hoped that she would marry a boy from the upper class and have a good house to live in.

However, this dream of hers was shattered when she learnt that her marriage had been fixed when she was barely a month old. The boy belonged to the Harijan community and was worse off than her family. As soon as she turned 16, she was married and sent to her in-laws' house in Bakutra village in Patan district. In the community a newly-wed girl's worth was judged in terms of the amount of dowry she brought with her. Her brother's wife had gained popularity when she brought with her a reasonable amount of dowry. In comparison she felt ashamed that her father had managed to give her only a few clothes and some pottery. Her new family included her father-in-law, her husband and his

*Acknowledgements: Adarsh Kumar, Asmita P. Pansare, Prajat Khare, Sirisha Tadepalli and Swati Agarwal.

two brothers. She considered herself lucky for not having to cope with a mother-in-law when she saw how young girls were bogged down by responsibility thrust on them by their mothers-in-law.

societal norms

Life did not have much to offer even after marriage as she started to work as a labourer right from day one. Her husband owned only a small piece of land and had to struggle hard to make ends meet. Gauri became pregnant when she was 19 years old. Societal norms did not allow a couple to go out together even to the dispensary for prenatal check-up. Gauri continued to perform her daily chores like fetching water even during her pregnancy. However, she fetched water at night, so as to avoid drawing attention to her swelling figure. At no point did her husband offer any support or comfort. A few days before her due date some of the village women came over to help her with the delivery. In her memory, those were the only days when she had some rest.

Her first child, a girl, was named Gita. The joy of becoming a mother was, however, short-lived as she had to perform her daily chores along with caring for the baby. The financial burden on the family increased. Her husband and his brothers earned a paltry daily wage of Rs 12 which was insufficient to feed six mouths.

change in fortune

Each day was no different from the other. However, one day something happened that completely metamorphosed Gauri's life. Reemaben, a member of the Self-Employed Women's Association (SEWA), came to the village in search of three women who would stitch and embroider eight *kurtas* for her organisation. Gauri heard about Reemaben from the villagers who referred to her as the lady from Ahmedabad who wanted her clothes stitched in the village. Since stitching and embroidery were part of the chores Gauri had been doing since childhood, she did not hesitate to volunteer her services.

She took up the work along with Badhiben and Raniben. They were so ignorant of the prospects being offered that the thought of receiving money for their work did not even occur to them. Reemaben provided them the raw materials and told them to complete the work within eight days. Having no contact with the outside world or with fashion, Gauri diligently worked day and night to do exactly as she had been instructed. When Reemaban came after eight days, she was extremely pleased with the work. She paid all the women Rs 150 each for the work they had done! Gauri could not believe her eyes. The amount was far more than what she had ever seen in her life. It was more than double of what her husband earned in a week.

new avenues

The news of the women earning so much money spread like wild-fire in the village. When Reemaben arrived with the next consign-ment of 12 *kurtas*, many women lined up for work. She wanted to give one *kurta* per person so that more women had a chance to earn. The task of selecting 11 other women was entrusted to Gauri. However, because of a severe financial crisis at home Gauri decided to stitch two *kurtas* herself and distributed the rest. She told the other women that Reemaben had given only 11 *kurtas*. She worked on the second *kurta* at night so that no one would notice. The amount of Rs 300 that she received lightened her financial burden.

As more women realised this opportunity to earn, the men be-came uneasy because they felt threatened and insecure. Their wives, who had never stepped outside the threshold of their homes, were suddenly earning in a few days what they managed to earn in months.

positive stand

As an increasing number of women enthusiastically participated in SEWA's activities, the organisation decided to provide professional training to women to make them self-reliant. The training programme included teaching the proper use of colours, threads and techniques of stitching and embroidery. However, the training programme was not organised in the village, it was held in another district. The men were reluctant to let their wives step out of the house, let alone travel to another village on work. The general perception was that people from the city were trying to lure away their womenfolk to work for them and would not let them return. While Gauri's husband shared the same view, her father-in-law was more progressive. He advised her not to waste her talent and encouraged her to join the programme. Initially, Gauri and three other women had to feign illness to get permission from their husbands to 'see the doctor'. Gradually, as the men saw how the training and meetings augmented the household income, they came around to the idea.

benefits of saving

As Gauri was assured of a steady income, she began to save Rs 5 from every Rs 150 that she earned per *kurta*. As with most daily wage earners in Bakutra, the concept of saving was a fantastic dream. Where the income was not sufficient even for one proper meal a day, being able to plan beyond regular meals and decent clothes gave Gauri a great sense of achievement. Gauri's efforts at saving were channelised in the right direction by Ayeshaben of SEWA. She made other women aware of the benefits of saving for a rainy day. Realising the importance of this hard-earned money, Gauri began to carefully plan her expenses and did not allow her husband to squander it on trivialities.

The prosperity of the village women changed the perception of those who shunned them earlier. For instance, the local grocer, who shooed them away from his doorstep earlier, began to invite them into his shop to try out new products. Even differences based on caste and religion began to whittle away.

awareness drive

In due course of time, Gauri realised her dream of educating her five children, particularly both her daughters. One of them studied till class 5 and the other till class 7. She worked to create awareness among the villagers regarding the importance of education. Each day brought new offerings to Bakutra as SEWA introduced them to concepts they had never heard of before. Insurance was one of them. Dharmishtaben launched the insurance drive in the village by involving 30 women in the insurance plan at a premium of Rs 30 per month. SEWA selected two women each to handle the crafts and savings activities. These women reported to SEWA's centre at Radhanpur. Thay were driven to organise the entire process themselves.

new initiatives

The next initiative was to offer loans of up to Rs 1,000 for the purchase of seeds. Five women in two groups availed of this loan and began to cultivate their land. SEWA's initiatives had a profound impact on Gauri and other women: they not only became self-confident, but also aware of their rights and importance. They could voice their opinion openly without depending on their husbands to bail them out of difficulty. The change in general perception was also apparent from the fact that women were involved in the decision-making process of the village panchayat. SEWA helped them broaden their vision by acting as an interface between them and the outside world. Gender discrimination began to diminish.

latest trends

Having won laurels for her dedication and sincerity to her work, Gauri was offered an opportunity to visit Africa and Bangladesh to represent SEWA. She interacted with many new people on an international platform. She gained exposure to international fashion trends that she could incorporate into her work back home.

SEWA has brought about a sea change in the lives of the people of Bakutra and the entire Patan district. Apart from providing employment to nearly one lakh women in the district, SEWA has done work in the areas of health and sanitation. The organisation has constructed water tanks in villages which provide clean and safe drinking water to the people and women no longer have to trudge miles in search of water. Besides, awareness programmes have been organised in areas like first aid, water harvesting, dairy manage-ment, salt farming and family planning.

Gauri has the responsibility of coordinating all the work in her village, right from procuring raw materials to marketing the finished product. Her work includes monitoring the distribution of payments totalling Rs 1 lakh (Rs 100,000) in six villages in the district. She earns between Rs 1,000 and 1,500 per month from embroidery alone. Her life is full of opportunities. She has bought a house in her name and owns cows and bullocks. She also owns a television and a tape recorder and is planning to buy a computer.

Realising the importance of her work, her family members share household responsibilities whenever she has to go out for meetings. Her daughter Gita is 19 years old and Gauri does not want her to get married for another 2 years. She is not rigid about not giving dowry but is clear that whoever marries Gita should transfer property worth at least Rs 10,000 in her name. Gita also works for SEWA; she manages the register for the 'Naya Ghar Yojna' which aims at providing new homes for villagers affected by the devastating earthquake of 2001. She and her sister earn between Rs 1,000 and 1,500 every month. One of Gauri's sons is studying in class 9 in a reputed school outside the village. Since he is good in studies, she wants him to continue his education.

'son of Gauriben'

Gauri has earned so much respect in the village that her elder son is referred to as the 'son of Gauriben' and not by his father's name, as is the custom in the region. For Gauri, the sky is the limit. She continues to be associated with SEWA and wants them to set up a branch of the SEWA bank in the taluka which will make loans and finances easily accessible to the poor villagers. She is willing to manage the activities of the bank. Despite an opportunity to move to the city, Gauri wants to stay in the village and help other women realise their dreams the way she was able to. She attributes her success to Reemaben and to SEWA. According to her, it was SEWA that helped her realise her potential and improve her life. For her, it is not the end of the journey. She is raring to continue on the path of personal growth while helping others start on the journey that she once embarked upon.

TURNING THE TIDE*

carefree childhood

The household was happy and celebrating the birth of a baby girl. Joumi was born into a large cohesive joint family in the small township of Kubernagar near Ahmedabad. The family was headed by her grandfather and included her grandmother, parents, uncle and aunt. She had five younger brothers and sisters. Her father was a contractor. The family led a simple but comfortable life.

Though she belonged to a conservative community, Joumi had the rare opportunity to study till class 7. The little girl was not unduly burdened by household responsibilities: she studied, played and learnt handicrafts from her grandmother. At times she took

*Acknowledgements: Adarsh Kumar, Asmita P. Pansare, Prajat Khare, Sirisha Tadepalli and Swati Agarwal.

care of her younger siblings or assisted in the household chores. Joumi was inspired by tales of the Prime Minister of India, Indira Gandhi. Having read about Mrs Gandhi in school, Joumi wanted to study a lot so that she could do something significant in her life.

growing up

Joumi's zeal to learn was not approved by the patriarchal system she lived in. Her grandparents were against higher education for girls. They thought it was enough that she could read letters and number plates on buses. Though her parents were open-minded, they could not go against the elders' wishes. After spending a couple of years learning patchwork, her grandparents decided it was the right time for Joumi to get married. At the age of 17 she was married to Jairambhai Rajgour from Mandotra village in Kutch district. Her opinion was not sought in the matter. She was not even sure what marriage really meant.

At the time of the marriage her husband was on the temporary payroll of the Gujarat state government. Her in-laws' family included Jairambhai's parents and sister. The change in family environment was drastic for Joumi. Having led a protected life, she suddenly found herself in a really difficult situation where she had to manage within a limited budget. She had to walk miles in search of firewood and water—chores that she had never done in her parental home.

harsh realities

That was not the end of her problems, however, Jairambhai lost his job shortly after marriage. The family's financial status was reduced to that of a daily wage earner. This was the first time Joumi was faced with an acute financial crisis. Her father-in-law, a conservative Pandit, could not manage a steady job because of his old age. An irregular income was not sufficient to support the family.

Despite all the hardships, Joumi did not complain or move to her parents' house. The emotional support provided by her mother-in-law and husband gave her the strength to take it all in her stride. She shared a very warm relationship with her mother-in-law. The older woman taught her to prepare 'bajre-ki-roti' which she had never eaten before. Their situation continued to deteriorate and a time came when they did not have money to even buy wheat flour for rotis. Jairambhai's elder brother worked outside the village, but the family never approached him because they did not want to burden him with their problems.

Joumi gave birth to a girl in 1984 in the midst of all these problems. Life was different as she had to travel long distances with her husband and her daughter to earn a living. Many people in Mandotra had to cope with this grim situation. Nearly every year there was a drought in the village. Farming was possible for just 4 months in a year and that, too, when there was rain. Mass migration in search of work was common. People accepted whatever work they got.

The following year Joumi got work at the Anganwadi centre in the village. This helped augment her husband's paltry income. For the first time she stepped out of the house alone. The need to take care of her family overcame her fear of conservative social customs.

SEWA team

Joumi worked in the Anganwadi for the next two years. As part of her job, she acted as a facilitator between the Anganwadi programme and the villagers. She had to go out and communicate with them on a daily basis. During one such community meeting she met a team from SEWA. SEWA's activities in Mandotra and the neighbouring villages centred on social causes. According to Reemaben, the general secretary of SEWA, from the beginning she found Joumi different from other village women: Joumi was vocal and confident in her interactions with the villagers.

In Mandotra, SEWA's focus was on solving the water problem along with a group of villagers called the 'Gram Pani Samiti' (village water committee). The villagers, considering Joumi's work in the Anganwadi, nominated her on this committee. Under this project, Joumi was sent to Baroda by SEWA to introduce her to the 'Vadodara Tippak Sinchan Yojna'. She also visited the Amul Cooperative Society in Anand. While working in Mandotra, SEWA realised that water was not the only problem in the village. An even bigger problem was unemployment. When Joumi learnt that SEWA was interested in making women self-reliant, she saw an opportunity and approached Reemaben with a plan for self-employment. She was aware that many women in the village knew some handicrafts and embroidery and thought that this skill of theirs could be used for self-employment. She approached Reemaben with some samples of her own work.

new avenues

Till then SEWA had focused only on embroideries. Joumi's fine patchwork impressed Reemaben, who asked her to convince more women from the village to join in the effort. Joumi first needed to convince her own family before motivating other women. She received full support from her husband and mother-in-law, though her father-in-law did not approve of the idea. Under the circumstances, her husband and mother-in-law not only encouraged her to take up this responsibility, but also assured her of their full support. Joumi managed to persuade 25 women to work on this project. She taught them patchwork for the next 6 months for which she was paid a monthly stipend of Rs 500. While she was working on this project, her mother-in-law took care of her three children and her husband helped her in every possible way.

The amount of work kept increasing as Joumi received bigger orders. Her income rose proportionately. The family's financial condition improved and the children could go to school. Other women who were part of the programme also began to earn well. A significant change that was seen in Mandotra after the inception of this programme was that the mass migration of earlier days declined to a great extent. People had regular employment opportunities in the village itself.

Apart from patchwork, Joumi learnt new skills like colour combination and designing, which were basically meant for export purposes. She taught these skills to other women as well. The job became increasingly tough and demanding. Joumi had to strike a balance between her house, training other women and learning herself. Instead of succumbing to pressure, she took it as a challenge and motivated herself.

Joumi was at the forefront when SEWA set up a salt-making unit in 1991 in the Rann of Kutch. Her work took her beyond the limits of Gujarat to Delhi, Mumbai and Bangalore. In 1994, she was appointed as the 'mantri', that is, the area chief of the Banaskantha unit of SEWA. She was also made a member of the SEWA business committee. Her job included representing SEWA at various exhibitions. Increasing business meant that she spent less time with her family. Joumi never faced any opposition from her family; in fact, they were proud of her.

exquisite work

Joumi continued to grow with SEWA. In May 1999 she was sent to France to represent India in a handicrafts trade fair. The French people saw for the first time such exquisite handwork. Joumi's responsibility was to demonstrate and explain how the work was done. She spent 2 months in France. In 2001, Joumi was sent to Washington DC, to attend a computer-aided designing workshop organised by the World Bank.

Joumi has come a long way over the last 16 years. Till date she has trained more than 500 women from 22 villages. Mass migration from these villages is a thing of the past and people's financial status has improved considerably. Twenty-five women with whom she had initially worked are also part of the various business committees of SEWA.

Joumi has set up her own computer centre in Mandotra and is involved in teaching women computer-aided designing. Her eldest daughter is married and the other children are pursuing their studies. She has a dream of her children carrying forward her strong association with SEWA. Joumi reveres Reemaben and gives her the credit for all that she has achieved in her life. According to her, SEWA is her family and she would like to work with it and contribute to it in whichever way she can for the rest of her life.

NURTURING TALENT*

On his way to Jamshedpur railway station, Ashwini was in a particularly low frame of mind. In a pensive mood, he recalled the day he had first arrived in the Steel City. He had been working in the AC division of Avion Networks (India) Pvt. Ltd for over a year. But everything seemed to have gone wrong during the last 6 months.

A production engineer, Ashwini had joined a core technical firm in accordance with his aspirations although he had lucrative offers from software firms, thanks to the boom in the information technology sector. Ashwini faced a seemingly impossible problem: he could be held responsible for losing the most valued client of his company.

positive start

Essel Steel, the largest industry in the region, supported the entire economy of the region. Almost 85 per cent of the population in and around Jamshedpur directly or indirectly depended upon Essel Steel for its livelihood. Most of the industries in and around Jamshedpur were either suppliers to Essel Steel or its outsourcing partners at various levels. Avion Networks (India) Pvt. Ltd, a

*Acknowledgements: Abir Kanjilal, Arvind Krishnan. Indranil Das, Nitin Kumar, Ratnakar Mani and Suman Nag.

wholly owned subsidiary of Avion Inc, USA, supplied industrial ACs and UPSs to Essel Steel. With product features technically superior to those of domestic companies, Avion was the default choice of Essel's management in spite of the premium it charged. Avion even offered 48-hour part replacement and maintenance warranties.

Ashwini took up his new assignment in Jamshedpur with his characteristic zeal. His job responsibility included providing technical expertise to the Jamshedpur unit and the neighbouring industries; a responsibility seldom entrusted to a junior engineer.

performance appraisal

From day one he visited the site frequently and insisted on regular feedback from the maintenance contractors. At the end of each day's work he would go through the feasibility report of Avion's expert. He enjoyed much credibility among not only the on-site managers of Essel Steel, but also his team members.

Aditya, his team leader, had a different perspective on how work should be handled. He strongly believed in an organisation-driven system as opposed to a people-driven one. He realised that the technical team had become overdependent on Ashwini. Every petty detail like fuse replacement and compressor pressure control required Ashwini's consent. He appreciated Ashwini's knowledge and sincerity but this went against his belief in a systems-driven organisation. Of late, this thought had begun to bother him but his own loss of technical acumen over the years prevented him from confronting Ashwini. According to him, Ashwini should have encouraged his team members to think for themselves rather than providing them ready-made solutions.

Aditya's predicament was reflected in Ashwini's mid-year appraisal. Though he scored high on technical and on-job responsibility, he was below par in team-building skills. Ashwini was taken aback by his appraisal. He had single-mindedly focused on his responsibility for the past 6 months but had never given a thought to team-building aspects.

On his return to the regional office in Jamshedpur, he appeared more passive. Aditya occasionally observed his cold response and tried in vain to talk to him. Ashwini began to devote more time to his team members rather than attending on-site calls. Aditya observed that this was not taken well by the managers of Essel Steel but thought that things would improve with time. Though Ashwini spent an appreciable amount of time with his team members, he lacked the ability to inspire a conversation on problem analysis. The discussion was invariably on petty organisational matters.

managerial reshuffle

To make things worse, a managerial reshuffle across various units of Essel Steel led to further dissatisfaction. On a few occasions part replacement took more than 48 hours. Ashwini knew that Essel Steel was a highly valued customer and any loss of credibility would not be perceived well even by the neighbouring industries. As a result, this year's target would be adversely affected. Ashwini's motivational level was at an all-time low and prevented him from inertia building up a relationship with the new managers. A letter of concern from Essel Steel to the regional headquarters brought Ashwini in the firing line. The equity he had enjoyed over the years was at stake but he had little explanation to offer. Even Aditya was caught between his belief and action. After the regional manager returned to Calcutta, Ashwini was summoned to the headquarters.

WINNING WAYS*

Jyotiraditya was known for achieving extraordinary results in every opportunity that came his way. He worked for the best brand in

*Acknowledgements: Atul Rohan Garg, Deepak Singh, Garima Gupta, Rashmi Wadhwa and Traptika Chauhan.

the industry. He was on the fast track to success after being selected for his company's corporate management development programme (CMDP). Popular with staff members and colleagues, he enjoyed a good professional rapport with the clients.

If everything was going his way, then why did he leave the company to pursue an alternative career?

about Jyotiraditya

Jyotiraditya graduated from one of the best B schools in the country. He was not an outstanding student but his leadership qualities set him way above his more intelligent classmates. Self-confident and fond of challenges, he was a good team worker. These very qualities made him an easy choice for companies during campus recruitment. Jyotiraditya finally accepted the offer from one of the leading business houses in the country. The flagship company, which functioned in the services sector, was looking for people to carry forward its success story through training in its CMPD. The programme was linked with its long-term strategic planning and formed a significant part of the company's growth.

The company was proud of its history, values and social responsibilities. Its commitment to business ethics was widely publicised and implemented. Recently, the parent business house had withdrawn from a government contract worth Rs 3,500 crores on grounds of upholding corporate values. Coming from a armed services barckground, Jyotiraditya appreciated the company's belief in its values and advocacy of corporate social responsibility. It had always been his ambition to work for such an organisation and he devoted himself to the work.

flying start

Jyotiraditya joined the corporate office at Mumbai. The CMDP started well and soon he was comfortable with the other management trainees. The programme was well developed and gave

Jyotiraditya ample scope to hone his managerial skills. The role of the participants of the CMDP was well defined. They were instrumental in the company's efforts to prepare for the future. The CMDP trained Jyotiraditya and his colleagues to implement the process of change that the company had planned to meet future challenges.

The company traditionally had a large workforce of skilled and semi-skilled labour. However, increasing market competition brought forth the need to reduce its overheads and hence, streamline the workforce. The emphasis was on efficient management and utilisation of human resources for achieving optimal output. To this effect, most of the top brass were also reshuffled, including the President and Vice President who had selected Jyotiraditya. At that time he did not attach much significance to the change.

Upon completion of the programme, he was appointed assistant manager and was deputed to New Delhi along with two other colleagues. The unit was important for the company because it generated the maximum revenue and had high profitability. Its annual sales exceeded Rs 10 crores, which was the highest in the market. The general manager inducted the new team into the unit. He, too, had been recently deputed from the corporate office and needed time to implement the designed strategy. He had identified certain internal elements that were disrupting the proper implementation of the organisational goals. This was also affecting the unit's and the organisation's profitability and credibility.

corporate goals

Without mentioning names, the GM stressed on not encouraging such disruptive elements and advised the three new recruits to work sincerely towards the larger organisational goal. Jyotiraditya was assigned to the core department that contributed to half the total revenue of the unit. He was one of the youngest managers in the organisation to have ever been entrusted such responsibility. He was very happy with the assignment and worked zealously to implement the new policies.

The age difference between Jyotiraditya and some of his staff members was as much as 30 years. Being accustomed to traditional practices, they put up stiff resistance to his work. Realising that the support of his staff members was crucial if he was to make any headway in the task at hand, Jyotiraditya spent much time establishing a rapport with the staff. He began by identifying key opinion builders within the department and brought them about to his way of thinking. Once the support of his staff was secured, he was able to put the managerial inputs received during the CMDP to effective use. Staff satisfaction increased, productivity went up and the cohesiveness of the unit also increased.

contradictions

While the department continued to progress under Jyotiraditya, he had trouble with his superiors. At one point he was required to report to six managers within the same department. The distinction in authority was not made clear to him. The designations were similar, two of them sharing the responsibility of the head of department and four being deputy heads of department. The only way he could interact with the general manager was by channelising his requests through all of them. Often there were conflicting orders from the various heads.

Personal agenda also disrupted the successful implementation of corporate policies. Each manager in charge had his informal group of supporters from among the staff members. With contradictory power lines emerging within the department, all Jyotiraditya and his two colleagues from CMPD could do was to distance themselves from the rampant organisational politics. Soliciting his superior's help even for operational issues such as financial sanctions became difficult without engaging in relationship management.

The environment continued to deteriorate. His two colleagues finally left the organisation; one chose to pursue higher studies and the other took up another job. Jyotiarditya felt increasingly isolated. Around the same time his job responsibilities increased:

he had to train 150 staff members of the department, he became the process owner for a customer satisfaction tracking system and in charge of another department. With the increased workload, he was barely able to keep track of his core department's daily activities. However, being unsure of his relationship with his superiors, he preferred not to talk to any of them about it.

letter of warning

One incident in particular affected Jyotiraditya adversely. Because of continued indiscipline of two staff members, he reprimanded them at the behest of one of the heads of department. When verbal warning had no effect, he issued formal disciplinary letters in their names. This was not appreciated by another head of department who was especially close to the two employees. He became increasingly hostile towards Jyotiraditya and finally had him transferred to another department.

The new department catered to a different market segment. Jyotiraditya had to learn the work all over again and also adjust to a new team. His additional responsibilities, however, remained unchanged. He found himself stretched to the limit. He lost focus and was unable to repeat his earlier success story. Not satisfied with the results, he decided to talk to his superiors. He hoped that they would understand his problem and assign a part of his additional responsibilities to someone else. However, his hopes were dashed. He was transferred to another department, with no change in his additional responsibilities. Besides, he no longer had independent charge of the new department and had to report to seven, instead of the earlier six, heads of department! The continuing intra-organisational politics added to his woes.

change

Jyotiraditya got some respite when one of the departmental heads was transferred. The new manager, Ajay, had earlier been with the unit's competitor. Ajay was a dynamic manager with a different outlook as compared with his predecessor. As a last resort, Jyotiraditya approached Ajay and got a patient hearing from him. After checking his track record and talking to his former colleagues, Ajay was convinced of Jyotiraditya's sincerity. Understanding his subordinate's problem he took it upon himself to guide Jyotiraditya through the difficult phase.

Jyotiraditya realised that continuing in the organisation was not helping his career. He seriously considered the idea of pursuing higher education and talked to Ajay about it. With Ajay as his mentor, he began to regain his confidence and his performance improved. Once he was certain that his performance graph had moved up, he decided it was time to leave on a winning note. He tendered his resignation and moved on to fulfil his dream.

8

❖

managing organisational crises

Expected Learning Outcomes

♦ *Identify various internal and external forces causing organisational crises.*

♦ *Analyse managerial behaviour in dealing with organisational crises.*

♦ *Understand institutional arrangements for preventing and managing organisational crises.*

♦ *Need for instituting the process of recovery from organisational crises including coping with trauma of managers experiencing crises.*

Organisations experience varying degrees of 'turbulence' at most stages of their functioning. Unexpected and unplanned events disrupt the normal routine and create situations of urgency. Unless handled properly and on a priority basis, such events can impact both the current and future functioning of the organisation. These events include accidents, death of employees or key executives, legal or ethical issues, disputes with clients or suppliers, labour–management fallout and negative media coverage (Kayes, 2003). Organisational systems are at times at the root of avoidable incidents such as practices of corruption or manipulation, gender biases or issues related to ethics. Organisational governance systems often fail to notice or institute a proper mechanism to prevent such incidents. These occurrences can lead to serious long-term negative consequences. Contingencies like workplace deaths, public dispute, or natural disasters may even create an emergency situation leading to a major shake-up from the top to the bottom of the organisation. In addition to these emergencies, organisations are also vulnerable to changes in the environment such as a sudden shortage in the supply of raw materials, a cash crunch, shifts in government policies, or a shortfall in electrical supply. Some of these changes can be anticipated and an alternative course of action planned before they take the toll on the organisation. Whether or not the organisation is aware of the likely upheaval, the effect of these factors can range from the organisation just dying out, through scrapping through the situation, to turning the emergency situation into an opportunity (James, 2003).

ORGANISATIONAL DYNAMICS OF CRISES

The systemic and management capacity to respond to crises arising from unexpected events varies from organisation to organisation. Believing that the environment can always be predicted is utopian (Lei and Slocum Jr, 2002). Most organisations at some point of their functioning experience contingencies and they have to draw on additional resources. The nature of operational and tactical systems that the organisational governance system puts in place for dealing with unexpected situations determines how well the organisation and its managers can cope with crises.

Some of the possible ways in which organisations may respond to crises include (Johnson and Macy, 2001):

- 'Ostrich syndrome': There is a disowning of the situation. The stakeholders tend to ignore the possibilities of any adversity happening to them and believe in 'It cannot happen to us'. The corporate governance as well as the top management presume in general smooth functioning of the organisation. Such organisations cannot easily accept the fact that they could encounter a problem that could shake them up and as a result do not make a realistic assessment of the reality. Investment to prevent and/or deal with any eventuality in future is often avoided. The syndrome is transformed into a feeling of defensiveness, where the emergent situation is looked at with suspicion (Slocum Jr, Ragan and Casey, 2002). Managers in such organisations may not have the competence to deal with the crisis. They often feel stressed out as they are not aware of any internal procedures or legal implications of a crisis situation.

- 'Disowning syndrome': Some organisations have a tendency to not accept the occurrence of a crisis as a natural process or due to organisational factors. They are so overwhelmed by the enormity of the situation that they are unable to respond functionally to the crisis. When the organisation chooses to disown a crisis, it may attribute the situation and its responsibility to the concerned manager(s). The top management or the organisational governance system that investigates the causes may attribute it to the ignorance or negligence of individual managers. The managers in such a situation feel stressed out and nervous about the likely consequences of the investigation. After the crisis many managers find it difficult to perform the expected managerial role. They continue to experience stress because of the apprehension that they may be held accountable and action may be initiated against them or may feel morally responsible for the crisis or feel loss of confidence in handling such a crisis again. This can impact the overall employee morale and productivity (Kast and Rosenzweig, 1985).

- Accountable/action-oriented governance system: Organisations that anticipate the occurrence of a crisis as a natural process are willing to take it in their stride within the organisational framework. Such organisations readily accept the crisis without an attempt to mechanically respond to it. The response is generally one that leads to maximum positive result with minimum long-term adverse impact on organisational and employee productivity. Proactive organisations make all possible provisions for anticipating crisis situations and develop preventive mechanisms as well as establish internal procedures for dealing with such crises. Managers in such organisations participate actively in handling the crisis situation and facilitate the process of diagnosing the causes of crisis for future prevention (Makridakis, 1996).

DYNAMICS OF ORGANISATIONAL CRISES

Any organisational contingency puts pressure on managers to tackle the situation in the best possible manner, with minimal adverse impact on organisational functioning. Senior managers and those in charge of teams in particular may bear the brunt of the crisis. They may feel threatened and unsure of the outcome as they may not possess adequate expertise or decision-making power to respond to the situation. In such a situation, the degree to which the organisation invests in them and trusts their potential becomes an important factor in their efficient handling of the situation. Managers may give various responses during the course of handling a contingency or a crisis situation.

- Managers feel extremely tensed and stressed, as they may not have the competence to handle the crises. Further, they may not be aware of internal procedures of handling crisis situations as the procedures for handling crises are not clearly split out in many cases. Similarly, they may not be aware of the legal procedures and the likely legal consequences in such a scenario.

- The non-availability of timely resources and guidance may multiply the negative consequences of a crisis. This may happen when the crisis is in a field location where the manager does not have access to immediate assistance. Being unaware of norms and procedures may heighten the impact.
- Managers become convenient scapegoats to organisational disowning of crisis situations. When there is a lack of transparency in the control system, the responsibility is shifted to the person most directly affected by the contingency.
- The manager feels that he is under a microscope, with each action and decision being minutely examined by the organisational heads for the likely consequences. There is lack of space and empowerment for independent and responsible handling of the situation and this may lead to stress, nervousness and burnout.
- The impact of the crisis may be traumatic and the manager may find it difficult to return to normal managerial functioning. He may feel morally responsible for the crisis, experience a loss of self-confidence, feel apprehensive about recurrence of the situation, or about being held responsible for what could have happened or for the steps taken. Such feelings arise more in a set-up where the functional work profiles are not clearly defined or the organisation is centralised in its functioning.
- The manager rises to the occasion and handles the situation efficiently and smoothly. There is minimum disruption of regular activities and the organisation is able to come out of the crisis without excessive waste of valuable resources.

Managing Organisational Crises

Organisations need to create appropriate organisational infrastructure to facilitate managers' ability to anticipate, prevent and/or handle a crisis situation. These may include:

setting up a preventive mechanism

One of the foremost aspects of managing organisational crises is to anticipate the possible risk areas that may cause contingencies. With foresight the impact of an unexpected event or occurrence may be minimised. Providing training in crisis management is effective in preparing managers to face contingencies whenever they arise. Regular monitoring of systems and structures developed to prevent or manage a crisis, knowledge of internal and external procedures to tackle emergencies, and the psychological and personal ramifications of a crisis are aspects that organisations have to take into account, not only for preventing a crisis, but also for coping with and managing one.

acceptance and transparency

Accepting the occurrence of the crisis is the first step towards handling it. Transparency is essential in keeping all concerned parties informed and part of the communication loop. The media or internal communication system are used to update the stakeholders of the objective situation and steps taken to handle it. Taking people into confidence and mobilising their support are important for effective crisis management. Ambiguity may cause roadblocks rather than solve problems and prolong the process of recovery.

speed of response

The speed of response to the crisis builds confidence in the concerned parties. At the first indication of an impending emergency, the organisation should from a crisis management team with special powers to take and implement decisions outside the regular organisational norms and procedures. When the employees and the concerned parties see the organisation as proactive in handling the situation, they also become more cooperative and result-oriented.

support mechanism

The crisis management team develops an on-site support mechanism during the crisis. The announcement of a possible relief package on the spot leads the affected parties to believe that they have support in coping with the emergency more effectively. The support mechanism should include a communication channel through which the organisation can reach out to the affected parties, continually assess the situation and make necessary adjustments. This prevents speculation, the spread of rumour and the affected party from assuming a confrontational approach.

avoid accusations

In several cases, the management makes accusations against the parties accountable for the crisis. Rather than focus on resolving the crisis, attention is diverted towards holding people accountable. In the absence of concrete evidence to support such claims, the situation becomes one of passing the buck. In the meantime, the crisis keeps mounting. Such attitudes may produce resentment and prevent employees from making active contributions to the resolution of the situation. A constructive way to handle such a situation is to initiate a process of sharing resources and building synergy to deal with the crisis.

post-trauma support and counselling

During the crisis organisations and individuals are engaged in fire-fighting. Trauma and fears emerge once the phase has passed and the situation is under control. The affected parties require sensitive support and counselling to help them overcome the traumatic experience and move on with their professional and personal lives. Systemic support provides a sense of security and is an important buffer against continued anxiety.

lessons from the crisis

After the crisis has passed, there is a need for introspection and analysis of the causes, responses and consequences so as to objectively assess the impact of the crisis and the capability of the organisation to respond to such contingencies. The core team draws lessons for better prevention and management of crises in the future. Rewarding key action and risk takers and contributors to the crisis management efforts serves as a motivator for continued initiative and for inspiring others to participate in organisational activities more enthusiastically.

CASES ON MANAGING ORGANISATIONAL CRISES

The three cases included here highlight the dilemma faced by managers in trying to avoid a crisis or who are confronted by a crisis and have to manage the situation efficiently. The associated stresses and pressure to produce optimal results mat lead to personal burnout, while maintaining organisational productivity.

In Recovery of the NPA, an anticipated crisis could precipitate the occurrence of communal riots in a village. A bank in the region had provided loans to villagers under the rural development policy. However, the lax recovery system led to a large number of defaulters. The communal sensitivity of the village coupled with the fact that several defaulters belonged to the minority community were additional hindrances in the process of recovery. In such a situation, the bank manager faced the unenviable task of implementing an effective recovery system without hurting local sentiments and while maintaining the bank's reputation.

The Drilling Camp describes work in a coal mine. The field supervisor was known for working well even under adverse circumstances. One day a worker died at the site in a freak accident and the locals got together demanding compensation for the bereaved family. They refused to let the body be cremated until their demands were met. Due to heavy rainfall in the area, the village was virtually cut off from the district headquarters. The field supervisor had to cope with the situation. The case discusses the helplessness of a manager in handling an on-site crisis.

Bhoomi Air Base discusses a crisis situation at an Indian Air Force base when some packages containing parts of a missile head were found to be missing. An enquiry revealed that the local people had indulged in antisocial activities in and around the base. They also trespassed on the security zone. The decision to fence the boundary was met by opposition from the villagers and the local politicians. The officer in charge even received a summons from the district court to explain the reason for fencing. Given the economic concerns and involvement of national security an amicable solution had to be found at the earliest.

REFERENCES

James, Constance R. (2003). Designing learning organisations. *Organisational Dynamics, 32*(1), 46–61.

Johnson, Douglas B. and Macy, Granger. (2001). Using environmental paradigms to understand and change an organisation's response to stakeholders. *Journal of Organisational Change Management, 14*(4), 314–334.

Kast, Fremont E. and Rosenzweig, James. (1985). *Organisation and management,* (4th edn). New York: McGraw-Hill.

Kayes, D. Christopher. (2003). Proximal team learning: Lesson from United Flight 93 on 9/11. *Organisational Dynamics, 32*(1), 80–92.

Lei, David and Slocum Jr, John W. (2002). Organisational design to renew competitive advantages. *Organisational Dynamics*, *31*(1), 1–18.

Makridakis, Spyros. (1996). Factors affecting success in business: Management theories/tools versus predicting change. *European Management Journal*, *14*(1), 1–20.

Slocum Jr, John W., Ragan, Cass and Casey, Albert. (2002). On death and dying: The corporate leadership capacity of CEOs. *Organisational Dynamics*, *30*(3), 269–281.

CASES ON ORGANISATIONAL CRISES

key learnings

♦ *Identify personal and situational conflicts that a manager experiences while performing duties.*

♦ *Diagnose the internal and external factors of organisational crises.*

♦ *Apply lateral thinking in dealing with various organisational crises.*

♦ *Assess the role of the organisation in managing crises.*

♦ *Suggest organisational mechanisms for prevention and handling of crisis situations.*

♦ *Present the framework for recovery process in the post-crisis situation.*

RECOVERY OF THE NPA*

Ramesh was getting ready for work on a winter morning in December 1992. As the branch manager of the Rahimpur branch of UBI Bank, he was the first one to reach office. After completing MBA from one of the premier B schools in the country, he had joined the banking sector as a trainee. Due to his hard work and competence, he quickly moved up the corporate ladder. Within 2 years of his initiation he had been promoted to senior manager. Recently, he had been promoted to branch manager. However, he was faced with a dilemma regarding the recovery of bad debts from his branch that had repercussions for his growth graph. There was pressure from above to solve the matter quickly. Deft handling of the situation was likely to hasten up his promotion as well.

total deposits

The problem began during the 1980s when the government had formulated the rural development policy. Under this policy banks in rural areas were to divert a part of their total deposits as loans to poor farmers without asking for collaterals. The scheme was aimed at reducing the rich–poor divide by providing capital for agricultural purposes to poor farmers. Located in a remote part of Uttar Pradesh, the majority of families in Rahimpur were below the poverty line and were likely beneficiaries of the scheme. The land was fertile, but productivity was low due to want of adequate capital for agriculture.

Though the scheme was targeted primarily at the farming community, it was seen as an opportunity by some to make a foray into the transport business. These people took loans to buy trucks that were plying on the Mumbai–Delhi highway. This group

*Acknowledgements: Prashant Jain, Samnak Ghosh, Shity Jain and Vandana Mehra.

included four brothers from the minority community, who were the highest defaulters, accounting for nearly 40 per cent of the bad accounts. Interestingly, a majority of the bank depositors were from Rahimpur.

Ramesh's predecessor, Atul, had made several unsuccessful attempts to recover the loans. He had sent notices to the defaulters to repay the loan amounts. Despite repeated notices, none of the borrowers had responded positively. Considering the fact that many of the villagers were illiterate, it was highly liekly that the notices were not even read or understood. Given the easy availability of loans, the villagers thought that the government was distributing 'free cash' that was not to be repaid. By the time Ramesh assumed charge, the situation had gone out of control. Only 1 per cent of the loans had been repaid, and the likelihood of recovering the balance seemed little. With a good track record in rural banking, this was the first time that UBI Bank found itself in such a situation. The pressure was on Ramesh to show that results would add to the bottom line.

The bank representatives who visited the defaulters' houses never found them at home. The standard response was that the person concerned was away on work. The fact that the bank staff usually made home visits at a fixed time made it easier for the villagers to avoid meeting them. Initially, Ramesh thought of confiscating the property bought with the loans. However, given the planning of the villagers, neither he nor the other bank staff ever saw the trucks to evaluate their worth.

The problems were aggravated by communal riots that had broken out a few weeks earlier. The police found that the riots were the handiwork of some external elements who had entered the village and arrested them. The situation was brought under control; but the riots had left their mark. Rahimpur was a minority dominated area; sentiments ran high and the prevailing tense conditions did not warrant the use of force to recover the loans. Ramesh's community was also the target of much hatred; particularly in view of the fact that the highest defaulters were from the minority community, Ramesh could not afford to take legal recourse and add fuel to fire. The four brothers were considered prominent opinion leaders in the village and any action taken against them was likely to take on communal overtones.

The village had a Collector and a police post. The people held the Collector in high esteem. He was considered the highest authority and everyone went by his judgement. He agreed to help Ramesh in recovering the loans if the latter devised some means of going about it other than using police force. He was apprehensive about using the police as it would lead to a fresh spell of communal disturbances. Since Rahimpur was a small village with traditionally a low crime rate, the police post had just one SHO and four constables. The SHO was viewed second only to the Collector in importance—even having tea with him was considered a status symbol.

All these considerations apart, using police force was likely to be perceived as a sign of weakness. Also, the time lag in the legal procedures would adversely affect Ramesh's chances of making a favourable impression on his superiors through a speedy solution. The question was how should he handle the situation deftly and with restraint, while showing optimal results?

THE DRILLING CAMP*

The sky was overcast, it had been raining incessantly for four days. Visibility was low and the road had become a rivulet. Though it was past 9 o'clock in the morning, life had come to a standstill in the remote village of Madhavpur. But not for Tushar Mehta; for him work took priority over other matters. The field supervisor for a government project and a workaholic, nothing could deter him from discharging his duties. Dressed neatly, he walked the distance from his house to the drilling site.

*Acknowledgements: Prashant Jain, Saunak Ghosh, Shity Jain and Vandana Mehra.

remote belt

The project had been commissioned by a public sector undertaking under the Ministry of Coal for integrated exploration of coal. As part of this project, the team was engaged in drilling to test the availability of coal in this belt near a major steel plant. The base camp was cut off from civilisation because of lack of communication facilities. It was home to about 90–100 staff members and their families. However, like Mr Mehta's, many of the staff members' families lived in the city, away from the hardships of everyday life here. His wife and son, who studied in class VII, lived in the city. As part of the welfare measures for the staff community, a well was being dug. The job of drilling and digging the well had been given to a contractor and Mr Mehta was in charge of the job. Work on the well was nearing completion.

The deadline for completing the drilling was only two days away; work had been proceeding on schedule till the rain ruined everything. Absenteeism had risen. Known for beating deadlines, Mr Mehta was under pressure for the first time. Because of his track record he had been chosen to handle the work in this inhospitable site and he had taken it up as a challenge to do a good job as always.

on-site tragedy

When he reached the site of the well, 8–10 workers were at work. The ground had become waterlogged and slippery because of incessant rains. An old contract labourer was sitting on the brick lining on the periphery of the well. Suddenly, he lost his balance and fell into the well. Two or three workers had the presence of mind to slide down the well with the help of ropes and pull out the unconscious man. Immediately a local registered medical practitioner was summoned. He examined the man and declared him dead. The cause of death could not be immediately ascertained: was it due the impact of the fall, or shock and cardiac arrest, or some other reason? It could be ascertained only after the post-mortem in the hospital in the town.

News of the death spread within no time in the camp. In spite of the torrential rains the base camp was crowded with the villagers. The village Pramukh and some of the local politicians also got wind of it. They rushed to the spot and lost no time in blaming the government agency and the field supervisor for the accident. They demanded suitable compensation for the deceased's family. At their instigation, the villagers asserted that they would neither allow the body to be taken out of the camp till job compensation was assured to the dependents of the deceased nor let the government employees leave. The local women got together and demanded adequate compensation for the widow. The workers suspended further work until some action was taken. The body was wrapped and placed on a folding cot under the shade. Mr Mehta tried unsuccessfully to convince the crowd that though it was an unfortunate incident, his team was not responsible for it. The contractor was solely responsible for the safety of his men.

blind faith

Evening turned into night without any let up in the rain. The situation was in limbo. The workers depended totally on the lobbying group to fulfil their demands. Being cut off from the headquarters gave the lobbyists a chance to come across more strongly. The local politicians had opposed the digging of the well right from the beginning. It did not serve their vested interests and reflected poorly on their efforts to develop the region. Money sanctioned by the government for similar projects in the past had been misused and they were worried about their misdeeds being exposed.

The Pramukh was an experienced man. He was a man of principles and stern conduct. He enjoyed good relations with Mr Mehta and was popular among the villagers. He also had a reputation amongst the lobbyists as a fair person. He was not sure of the politicians, but during the few times he had interacted with them in the past, they had not appeared hostile to him. On the management side, Mr Mehta enjoyed a very good rapport with his bosses. Though he did not want to take advantage of this, deep within he knew that in the worst of circumstances the top authority would support him.

Nevertheless, he was hesitant about certain issues. While his superiors would trust him, he ought to discuss the issue with them before taking a decision. The main problem was the rain. In the absence of any scope for communication with the head office the situation assumed monstrous proportions. All roads were inundated. Even if someone was ready to travel, selecting a reliable person was critical. The other problem was the custody of the corpse. Unless a decision was taken soon, the body would begin to decompose, leading to a whole set of new problems. Besides, there was the issue of compensation. There was no policy for cash compensation: either compensation had to be given in kind or the policy had to be sidestepped. Given the strong lobby group, the decision had to be fair to stand any chance of acceptance. The only other possibility was to drive the office jeep himself to the nearest town 13 km away and talk to his superiors about the issue.

Considering the sensitivity of the issue, what would you do in Mr Mehta's place?

BHOOMI AIR BASE*

As Group Captain S K Verma addressed the gathered staff, he appeared tense and preoccupied. He had called a meeting to discuss the latest developments at the Bhoomi air force base near Shaila, Uttar Pradesh. The safety of the air base was in question and he wanted to find the best solution in the shortest possible time.

*Acknowledgements: Prashant Jain, Saunak Ghosh, Shity Jain and Vandana Mehra.

about Verma

Verma had joined the Indian Air Force as a fighter pilot 23 years ago. He was part of 'Operation Vijay' at Kargil and had flown many daunting missions. His leadership and courage inspired many of his colleagues and juniors. Often administrative and management crises were averted as a result of his efficient handling of the situation. He shared a good rapport with the Defence Secretary, Mr Thomas, in Delhi.

The Bhoomi Air Force station is spread over an area of 1,000 acres. It is a transport base and provides logistical support to the troubled northwest sector of the country. The staff capacity is 500. In the vicinity lies the small village of Shaila with a population of 5,000. The main source of income is sugarcane cultivation and cattle grazing. Literacy levels are low. The village lacks basic amenities like clean drinking water and sanitation and there are no paved roads connecting the village with the outside world.

internal problems

Reporting late for duty and absenteeism were major problems at Bhoomi. There was evidence of corruption at the lower levels. The bills for vegetables of the staff mess showed rates nearly 50 per cent higher than the market price. Stocktaking revealed that 150 bottles of wine were missing from the pantry. Verma was convinced that the differential behaviour towards officers and non-officers was at least partly responsible for such incidents. He objected to the prevailing British system of separate toilets and CSD canteen queues for commissioned officers and non-officers. According to him, many of the airmen at the station were highly qualified and talented and needed an environment conducive to the development of their potential. He therefore relaxed some of the rules.

missing missile head

Matters came to a head when one of the boxes carrying a missile head was found missing. Apart from the economic loss, it was a grave security breach. If the matter was not resolved quickly, a high level enquiry would be instituted and Verma would be held accountable. Flying Officer Manish Aggarwal was the duty officer for the armoury when their incident occured. He asserted that he completely trusted his staff and did not suspect anyone from his department. The only other people who handled the weaponry were the MT section that transported them and truckers from a local transport company owned by the villager Naseer.

problems galore

One day Verma had gone for an evening walk when he overheard some men discussing a chain-snatching incident involving an officer's wife. The case was later reported to the police. Some airmen also reported that villagers often trespassed on the security zone and misbehaved with the guards. A few cases of eve-teasing, hooliganism and stealing of the mess food had been noticed. As the base was in an open area, the village cattle at times strayed into the prohibited space.

A decision had been taken to develop the base into a classified information centre and Verma had been given the charge of developing it. Such incidents detracted from the required level of security and seclusion. The Air Force police were unable to catch the culprits as the villagers were not forthcoming with information. Verma thought that fencing the boundaries would prevent trespassing and solve the issue. He discussed it with his deputy, Squadron Leader M. Batra, and they decided to start work on fencing immediately.

stern step

A few days later some people from the village, led by the sarpanch, met him. The sarpanch was opposed to the idea of fencing of the base. He argued that if the boundary was fenced the farmers would have to walk another 2 miles to reach their fields. The cattle could not go so far and precious time would be wasted.

Verma did not want to take any step that would upset either the villagers or the basemen. He was aware that the issue was blown out of proportion by a handful of trouble-makers. The villagers were not antagonistic towards the base staff. Verma realised that he could neither take any stern measure that would aggravate the plight of the villagers nor could he ignore the safety issue of his men and the base.

Some pressure groups in the village threatened to file a legal suit against the base. They argued that since the land did not belong to the Air Force, it had no right to fence it. These groups included some local politicians as well. This meant that Verma had to tactfully handle the issue since any wrong move was likely to assume political undertones.

At the time there were communal tensions in the country. Politics in Uttar Pradesh had become volatile and the public had given a fractured mandate in the last election. Local politicians enjoyed tremendous power in a small village like Shaila which was Muslim dominated and, the local political leader was also a Muslim. This prevented Verma from taking any swift and strong action.

the land deal

Verma asked the administration office to procure the land deal report from the Ministry of Defence. According to the report, the government had transferred the land to the Air Force, but as the deal was very old, there was no substantial proof. Even after the base had been set up villagers had continued to use the land and so far the Air Force had not had any problems with this.

Verma was in for a shock when he was summoned by the district court to give a clarification on the issue. He saw through the tactic. Given the long-drawn-out legal procedures in India, the filing of the case was an attempt to help the villagers to continue their use of the land. Verma could have pursued the case further, but he could not afford the time that would entail.

difficult choices

After 4 hours of deliberation the group came up with several possible options:

Relocate the village.
Continue fencing.
Give compensation to the villagers.
Let the law decide.

A realistic assessment of these options did not reveal a rosy picture. The villagers had some religious sentiments attached to the place and were unlikely to relocate. Besides, this would involve huge costs and approval from the state and central ministries. Giving compensation to the villagers affected by the fencing was not within the purview of the base. Continuing with the fencing under the present conditions was likely to exacerbate the situation.

Legal recourse seemed to be the most practical option. However, Verma was sceptical about a quick solution to the case in the court of law. The urgency of the matter rendered this solution impractical. Besides, given the length of time elapsed since the land transfer, the Ministry had been unable to supply him with the complete requisite documents. The roadblock created by pressure from local politicians and human rights activists was another deterrent.

Index

❖

About the Authors

❖

Gautam Raj Jain is Senior Professor and Head of Organisation Development, Mudra Institute of Communications, Ahmedabad (MICA). He has held various academic positions in premier management schools like the Indian Institute of Management, Ahmedabad, the Goa Institute of Management, and Entrepreneurship Development Institute of India. He has also consulted with a number of international organisations such as PWC, ADB, UNIDO, ILO, UNDP and the EU and a number of corporate sector companies. Dr Jain has 27 years of academic and training experience and has conducted numerous training workshops in India and abroad. He has co-authored two books and published several papers in reputed journals and books.

Atul Tandan is the Director, Mudra Institute of Communications Ahmedabad (MICA) and has 34 years of professional experience in the industry and the academia. While the last nine years have been exclusively committed to post-graduate management education, his previous industry experience saw him in senior management positions with organisations such as Hindustan Lever, Cadbury, Bajaj Electricals and JL Morison. He is an active member of leading management associations in India and is currently the Chairperson of the Advisory Board of Studies for the K.C. College of Management Studies, Mumbai. Atul Tandan continues to garner contemporary understanding of the industry through consulting and holding honorary responsibilities as a board member in several companies in the pharmaceutical, FMCG, media and publishing sectors.